ORIGINAL FLAVA

ORIGINAL FLAVA

CARIBBEAN RECIPES FROM HOME

CRAIG AND SHAUN McANUFF

BLOOMSBURY PUBLISHING
LONDON · OXFORD · NEW YORK · NEW DELHI · SYDNEY

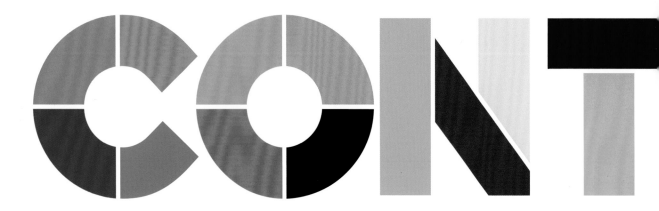

CONT

All Day Flava   26

Bring da sunshine to your day from early marnin'
to brunch, lunch and dinner

Pon di Side   56

Flavalicious sides, good nuff to nyam on their own,
plus our special home-made sauces

Street Food, Beach & BBQ   94

Snacks and meals with the carnival and beach vibe,
inspired by stalls and cook shops around the Caribbean

DINER DELUXE RESTAURANT & REST STOP

FREE DELIVERY
FREE Wi-Fi
CALL US TODAY
TEL (1876) 770-8913

INTRODUCTION

We're two brothers from South London sharing easy recipes from home. We started by filming recipes in our nan's kitchen in London, gaining hundreds of thousands of online followers and having a #1 self-published book – crazy, eh? Now we've explored the food stories of the streets and authentic flavours on a journey to our family's homeland of Jamaica – *the Original Flava!*

Our motto is EAT: we make our recipes Easy, Accessible and Tasty. We want to give you platefuls that taste like Nan's food, and we also like to twist it up a likkle to give dishes our modern spin. Caribbean food looks so good on the plate that you might ask *'How am I going to make that?'* We're here to show you how, making it easy like one-two-three.

In this book you'll find recipes jus' like back ah yard. There are recipes for all day, everyday food – breakfast, brunch, lunch and dinner; dishes for big gatherings with family and friends; the all-time Caribbean classics of Ackee and Saltfish and Curry Goat, and other island favourites such as Garlic Butter Lobster. Our chapter of Ital vegan recipes is inspired by Rastafarian culture, and there's another on the snacks and meals you enjoy at Carnival, roadside stalls and fish shacks. There's sweet food and drinks to hit the sweet spot and Saturday soups and stews for deep-down comfort. Stout Stew and Rum Punch four ways?

Throughout, we've been inspired by our time travelling in Jamaica, where we cooked with our family, ate jerk chicken, sipped pon a likkle rum and talked to the locals about the secrets of Caribbean cooking.

Jamaican food is so vibrant, lively, exciting and full of the influences from different cultures that make the island so wonderful. You look at it, smell it, you want to eat it! Most important of all is the togetherness it brings – the same happiness we have with our family. We want to share this joy, a testament to the culture of Jamaica that's full of fun, fantastic FLAVAS, and the stories behind the food. So get your ingredients, turn on a likkle music, and let's get cooking!

YA MON!

MEET SHAUN

Growing up in a Caribbean household, cooking has always been a massive part of my life. Mum loves bringing people together with food, and she cooked for us at home every day, after work. Coming in, it'd be *'Where's Mum?'* and she'd be in the kitchen. I wanted to see what was going on and be part of it. So I helped out with kitchen tasks for her, as well as for my nan, setting the table and taking dessert to serve to everyone.

I got used to the sweet-smelling recipes that woke me up out of my sleep. Easter time was my favourite. Grandma would make fried fish and plenty of carrot juice to wash it down – delicious. And how could I forget Christmas? We had so much food and drink – sorrel and Guinness punch filled up the fridge – along with the turkey and the Christmas ham. I wanted to know how to make everything, so over the years I watched and learned, taking it all in.

What I came to understand was the process. Food isn't just about cooking but everything that leads up to it: the shopping; getting the right goat meat with the bone, because that's where all the flavour is; having a relationship with the butcher and fishmonger; and details such as soaking the peas in advance to make them cook quicker and have the best texture.

When I left home to go to uni, I started cooking properly for myself. I'd make meals for my flatmates, and do my signature chicken wings for my friends' annual BBQ. Grandma and Mum instilled in me: *'Make sure you season overnight and use all the seasonings you can find!'* That's how you get all the FLAVA. When I went to work, I'd come in on Monday with leftover Sunday dinner – the Rice and Peas we had every Sunday without fail. I'd eat that with a selection of flavaful meats, and my colleagues would smell it all and ask who'd made it for me. They were just the meals I grew up learning how to cook – stew chicken, dumplings, plantain.

Then my brother Craig and I started combining food with social media. I'll never forget the day: it was April 2016. We'd see queues of people in our high street buying Jamaican food. I thought, people love this so why don't we go round to Nanny's and film a video of how to make it? We picked the spiced-bun bake, Bun and Cheese – a recipe every Jamaican loves. We researched, got tips from Nan and made a one-minute film. It went viral. That's how we started our business: cooking, showing and sharing Caribbean home-cooked food on the plate and online.

Now we help people all around the world to make delicious Caribbean recipes at home – for family, friends, boyfriends and girlfriends, husbands and wives, children and adults. As well as cooking, I've always enjoyed helping others and done voluntary work in hospitals and schools, as well as working in care homes. Through Original Flava, I'm able to inspire kids to learn to cook and to help support disabled people to eat well and have a better quality of life. Love and food bring everyone together.

MEET CRAIG

We had a good upbringing, close family, great friends. That said, I had challenging times through school. I was never the bad boy, but I knew a lot of people around South London and had a strong core friendship group that became a gang, which led to a few too many scary moments – the last one being approached by someone with a gun. That signalled the turnaround for me. I knew this wasn't the life I wanted and so I chose not to follow it. I guess it was willpower and wanting to make my family proud of me.

I'm a graphic designer. The way I cook reminds me of the creative process, making a hearty meal from small ingredients. Taste plays a huge part; I loved eating growing up, still do now. With food, the unity and feeling it brings to others make it so special. I was working on a project on Caribbean drinks at uni and said to Shaun, '*Let's do something together.*' We're different but adjusted to one another and we know each other so well – we shared a bunk bed when we were boys. We come together and it just works. Like all brothers, we have our disagreements, but after 30 seconds or so, it's all good!

The support we've received from followers has been overwhelming. We call them our family because we share special occasions online, like how I recently got married (big up di wifey!), everyday life, reminiscing about growing up in a Caribbean household in the UK – especially when we're chillin' at our grandma's, as she tells us stories about the past. I don't see her as my Nan; I see her as one of my best friends. We go over and talk, have a joke together. She has a lot to say and it stays with you, a bit like a guide throughout your day. Maybe that's what helped me not to follow the gang lifestyle back in the day. One of her favourite sayings that I've held onto is, '*If you want good tings ya nose affi' run.*' It means you've got to work hard if you want to succeed.

For me, when you have a feeling about food, it's not only because of the taste, it's also the inner story. Jamaicans have a deep history. Food is relaxation, fun, solidarity and togetherness. I'm in awe of the creativity of Caribbeans and how they first cooked their soups from things thrown away by slave owners and made them into dishes. Afro-Caribbean people can take something that's seen as oppression and turn it into something beautiful. Same with food, lifestyle, clothes, ideas, business, music. Throughout history, our outlook has been to innovate rather than be defeated.

Since starting Original Flava in 2016, it's been an amazing journey so far. My brother and I have worked hard, doing it ourselves, right from when we used the little money we had to buy a basic camera to film our first video. To be in the position we're in now is mind-blowing. We want to inspire youngsters to see that you really can achieve anything you set your mind to and work hard for.

We've taught people worldwide to cook our food and we can't wait to bring authentic Jamaican food to your kitchen!

MEET NANNY

I was born in Redlands in Clarendon, Jamaica, and lived in the countryside, where everyone was friendly and my people had a lot of land. My dad leave us for six month to cut cane to make some money, and in the other six month he come home to plant yam, banana, gungo (pigeon peas), corn and dasheen (taro) for us. Before school, I had to go to the river and catch water in a tin to fill up the barrel for my mum. She cook over fire, and she walk down the hill to bring me lunch, then we eat together before I go back to lessons.

I came to London April 1956, when I was 21. It was on the plane and I paid £85 – it was £75 on the boat because it took three weeks. When people arrived in winter, them couldn't find their place because of this dark fog. I got married a year later in Brixton Town Hall – a very nice wedding mon and we had nuff big-up food, like Curry Goat and Rice and Peas and all dem tings deh.

Times back then was very tough. There used to be signs that said *'No Blacks or Irish allowed'*, so we couldn't go to certain places. We had to stay in a house with five other people we didn't know, sharing the same toilet, bathroom and kitchen. You had to wake up really early so you could use the cooker first otherwise you had to wait a long time, and you dropped 10p in the gas to make your Saturday soup to feed the family. We all used to go to the market together to shop, and food brought us all together. Our room in Geneva Road cost about £1 a week back then, and this and Somerleyton Road were the baddest roads in Brixton – a lot of trouble – but now it's so nice. Times have changed!

We bought our first house in 1970, in Balham, and stayed for 20 years. Food was a big part of my memories there, with all my children and grandchildren, especially at Christmas and birthdays. During the six-week summer holidays the kids would stay with us and they always loved cornmeal porridge in the marnin, and the family come over on Sunday for lunch.

I had seven children, and at the same time worked in school, hospital, laundry. It was hard at first, but I just keep on going. Now I've got 13 grandchildren, and it's nice growing them up and to see how much stuff is going on now. When I can help, I help. When Shaun and Craig come round, we talk like big people even when they were likkle. Because they understand, they're not stupid. I tell them what's to come in life. They come in the kitchen more and more, and when you think them not looking, they take it in – and that's how it goes!

And when the family come round, I make a whole 'eap a food. We made so many memories of all the children dem. They, and God, were my strength! His grace and mercy brought me through.

JAMAICAN JOURNEY

Our journey was to find our roots and family, and to get to know more about the food and its history. We wanted to see how the locals cook, and to learn about the fresh fruit and veg and the authentic jerk process. And we also wanted to understand and experience the way food brings everyone together, along with the differences and connections between Britain and the Caribbean.

Craig had been to Jamaica once, when he was 17, and Shaun never – but our parents have been a lot. They always said how we'd love it, because of the sense of home (being the birthplace of our grandparents) and our love of cooking. Everyone knows about food in Jamaica – even little kids. It's a way of life, and a source of income for communities who cook and sell to provide for their families. If you have a conversation with Jamaican people, you can't not talk about food.

When we stepped off the plane, it was 30°C. But there's always the cooling ocean, and then suddenly you get huge tropical clouds and bursts of refreshing rain. Tourists tend to stay in the resorts – you can't blame them as Jamaica has some of the most beautiful beaches in the world – but our intention was to explore the real Jamaica. We were taken around by family, or the hilarious taxi drivers we met, Nigel and Norris da' Bawse (Boss), who swiftly became friends. With them, we mingled with neighbourhood communities all around the island, from Montego Bay to Clarendon. Wherever we went, everyone told us about food like they've got a recipe book in their head – it just rolls off the tongue.

At the very heart of our journey were visits to the homes of our father's family,

the McAnuffs, and, on our mum's side of the family, to Nanny Mitchell's childhood home.

Spicy Hill is where the McAnuff land is. As we drove up there, through the countryside of Trelawny in the centre of Jamaica, the reason for the name became clear – there's land filled with scotch bonnets, and thyme and spices growing everywhere. It's also the same parish where historically some of the Maroons were located – the escaped slave communities that were the originators of the jerk process.

As you enter Spicy Hill, you see the family's church, where our great-uncle was the pastor, and the family house right next to it – no excuse to be late then! Grandad was one of nine, and many of them left Jamaica to get work in other countries. There were all the photographs of our family up on the wall – it was an intensely happy moment looking at their faces and our past. Then we went to see their graves, up near the old family house. It's because of them that we're here. The legacy. Seeing their names and our last name. We're continuing the name and bringing it to food and bringing families together over meals. We wonder how they'd feel about their great-great-grandchildren, living in London, doing a book about their home. We met so many

Jamaicans who were proud of their food and love to see it enjoyed around the world, so hopefully we are making them proud.

We were hosted by our grandad's sister, Auntie Eloise, and our cousin Hopie at their home in Kingston. This was a special family welcome. Every morning Auntie Eloise came with fresh saltfish fritters, hard dough bread, boiled banana and dumpling and cook-up mackerel; then a range of teas and hot chocolate on a little serving tray.

On Saturday morning, a lady who helps Auntie Eloise at church accompanied us to the biggest market in Jamaica to shop for fruit and veg – Coronation Market in downtown Kingston. We were driven by a family friend, Norris, who warned us, without getting too heavy, about the pickpockets in the area that surrounds the market, aka The Gully. However, the market itself was far from dangerous, and was instead filled with welcoming vendors and with a warm sense of community love – a wonderful sight and experience.

When we got back to the house, Eloise made us chicken foot soup, yes, foot – not for everyone! We have chicken soup at home, and at church there's probably foot in

there because it's got such a good flavour, but we'd never actually seen it. In Jamaica, they're everywhere, and it's frowned on to say you don't like them. Also, when offered food by elders you can't say no, so to remain respectful, we pretended to

KINGSTON, JAMAICA

eat the chicken feet in there, bobbing about among the vegetables and dumplings. Saturday soup is such a big thing in Jamaican culture – you've got to have a soup on a Saturday, even in a hot country. It's something you can make in the morning and share with everyone who comes over at the weekend. For us, Auntie Eloise had made the ultimate Sat'day soup – YAH MON!

The next day we went to church in Kingston. Although thousands of miles away, it was so much like the old-school Pentecostal church where we grew up and everybody was Jamaican. In both countries, you have to be well dressed – men in best shirts, maybe with a tie, women perhaps in hats. The order of service and tambourines were the same, and then, of course, come the announcements. Everyone's trying to get on the mic! Eloise had told the church all about her family coming from London; as new guests, we stood up and people clapped – they love to see visitors. Black churches are very welcoming and very family orientated; they help to keep families together.

Sunday's a big day because you go to church – and while the service is going on,

you're thinking about the food at home! Even the preacher says, *'You can now go home to nyam your food.'* Our mum leaves the peas for her rice and peas soaking and comes back to finish it off. When we got back from church in Kingston, it was us who cooked a Sunday meal for the family: curry chicken, rice and peas, callaloo, breadfruit, plantain, avocado (or 'pear', as they call it) – as Nan would say, *'A whole 'eap a food!'* It felt like home in Eloise's kitchen, with the kitchen prayers up on the wall and gospel music playing as we cooked.

It wasn't until the last day that we made it up to Nanny's old home – her family's land in Redlands, up in the hills of May Pen, Clarendon. Uncle Wollie, Nanny's oldest son, lives there with Nan's brother Albert and his daughter Doretta and her

REDLANDS, CLARENDON

family. He's of a certain generation without a phone line or mobile signal, so it took a while to contact them and even longer to get there. It was far, far, far, far. We went up mountains, and the roads were so narrow with cars coming both ways. We'd never been up a hill so steep. One little hit of a rock on the road and you could easily tip over. It was a ten-hour round-trip journey, and raining in a tropical torrent on the way back. Driver Nigel was praying as he drove through potholes that had become lakes.

Nanny's family have a lot of land on a rocky hill. There it was, a big yellow building on its own, in Nanny's yard, where she grew up. A lot of people come to buy food from the garden: breadfruit, sugar

cane, mangos, oranges. They've got hogs and goats roaming free, chickens running around going cock-adoo and a special barn for eggs. The garden was like a vegetable market. What we would give to have access to incredible veggies and fruit like that!

To get some fruit, Uncle Wollie gave us a long bamboo stick and said, *'If yuh want it, fetch it yuself!'* As we chewed just-cut sugar cane and ate tangerines from the trees, we talked about family. We saw how Nanny lived and what she would have done if she'd stayed. We could have lived that life and been living there if Nanny never came over from Jamaica to Britain. She made that journey. Nanny tells us all the time that when she left here to come to London, her mum told her: *'You're a good person with a good heart, and everything you do is going to be blessed.'* And boy, was she right.

Our own journey to Jamaica took us deeper into what we do. We saw that food is a big way of life out there – they are passionate about what they cook and eat and make it their own. Nothing's really canned or processed; it's fresh from the tree and the ground. We thought we knew about food, but now we know so much more. It made us feel connected to our roots, our food, our people.

Jamaica is so much more than a tropical island and we understood that by being there. The people may not have a million pounds but they see life positively. The sun's shining, they've got food to eat. If you have a good meal, it puts you in a good mood. Eating is making good times and good vibes. That's an attitude anyone can share when they cook and enjoy Caribbean food and experience Da' Flava.

INGREDIENTS

ACKEE The national fruit of Jamaica and part of the national dish of Ackee and Saltfish, this unique fruit is eaten in savoury dishes. Enjoyed fresh in Jamaica, it is always sold in cans in the UK. Sometimes described as being similar to scrambled eggs because of its look and texture.

ALL-PURPOSE SEASONING A mixture of spices, including black pepper, pimento and garlic, this is used as a short-cut way to flava up food.

AVOCADO Known as 'pear' in Jamaica, where bigger types are grown than we get in the UK. Eaten for breakfast and at other meals with rice.

BANANAS Yellow and green bananas are used, with the unripe green banana boiled and eaten as a starchy food, or as part of hard food (see opposite).

BEANS AND PEAS Pigeon or gungo peas, kidney beans (we call them peas when they're in soup or Rice and Peas), black-eyed peas and yellow and green split peas are commonly used in Caribbean dishes as a staple protein.

BREADFRUIT Rich in vitamins and starch, which transforms to sugars when very ripe. The unripe fruit is roasted, baked, fried or boiled and served as a staple side dish, rather like potatoes.

CALLALOO A popular Caribbean leafy vegetable, eaten like spinach or kale.

You can buy it fresh near Caribbean communities, or canned elsewhere.

CHICKEN As well as the usual chicken pieces, such as leg and thigh or wings for Jerk Chicken, we also like to use chicken back – the remains of the chicken once it's been jointed – for flavasome soups.

CHO CHO A tropical plant that is native to Central America, with a pear- or oval-shaped fruit, cho cho is also called chayote and christophene. Mainly used in soups or salads.

COCO BREAD A slightly sweet bread that is used for sandwiches, or with a Jamaican Patty inside.

COCONUT Green when young, with delicious coconut water inside to drink and jellied flesh to eat. You mostly get the brown, older coconuts on sale in the UK.

COCONUT MILK Sold in cans or made by blending shredded coconut and warm water, then straining off the liquid.

COCONUT OIL An option as a cooking oil, with a nice flavour.

CORNMEAL Meal made from dried maize and a common staple food, ground to fine, medium and coarse consistencies. Mostly used for Cornmeal Porridge, but also in cakes, puddings and dumplings, such as Festival.

CURRY POWDER A mixture of chilli powder, ground turmeric, coriander, cumin and other spices, this is a key ingredient in Curry Goat, Curry Chicken and other dishes such as our Curry Tofu.

FRUIT Tropical fruits such as mango, pawpaw (papaya), passionfruit, guava, soursop, sweetsop (custard apple) and many others are used to make Caribbean juices and are also eaten fresh and ripe.

GINGER Jamaican ginger has a reputation for quality and is especially popular in ginger beer and in our curries.

GOAT A prized meat, most often eaten in the classic Jamaican dish of Curry Goat. Mutton can be used as a substitute.

HARD FOOD A mix of starchy foods, such as green bananas, yam and boiled dumplings, that is eaten alongside other dishes. Also known as 'provisions'.

JERK SEASONING A tasty mix of spices, including fresh thyme, pimento and chilli, that is part of our jerk dishes.

LIME Used more often than lemon in Jamaica, including for 'washing' meat and seafood before cooking.

MACKEREL Canned mackerel is a staple storecupboard fish used in dishes such as Mackerel Rundown or Cook-Up Mackerel, or else eaten fresh.

MOLASSES A by-product of the sugar-making process that is used in sweets and cakes.

NUTMEG AND MACE Nutmeg has a lacy outer shell called mace. The nutmeg is grated into dishes such as porridge and the milder mace can be used whole or powdered to infuse sweet or savoury dishes.

OKRA A popular vegetable with a sticky texture, used in many vegetarian Ital soups.

OXTAIL The tail of cattle that is made into a popular slow-cooked dish. It takes up to three hours to become tender but is worth the wait. We prefer small or medium pieces. Best eaten with Rice and Peas or steamed white rice.

PIMENTO One of our most typical spices, sold both as whole dried berries and as a ground powder. Known as 'allspice' in the UK because its flavour is like a mix of cloves, cinnamon and nutmeg. Whole pimento berries are used in recipes such as Rice and Peas and meat dishes to give the recipe a flavaful aroma.

PLANTAIN Cousin of the banana but never eaten raw. Used when green, semi-ripe (with a mottled skin), or as we like it, ripest and sweetest (with a black skin). Commonly fried or boiled – or even made into fries.

PUMPKIN Our pumpkin has a green skin and bright orange flesh with a great flavour. Mostly used in Saturday soups and curries, butternut squash is used as an alternative.

RICE A staple of Caribbean food, in Jamaica this is part of the classic dish of Rice and Peas or cooked on its own. We typically use long-grain or basmati rice.

SALTFISH Part of Jamaica's national dish, Ackee and Saltfish. The easiest kind to prepare is sold in packets –it needs to be soaked in water or boiled to remove the excess salt. Best eaten with ackee or callaloo and served with dumplings or green banana.

SCOTCH BONNET This classic chilli pepper is used in many of our dishes. It has a distinctive and delicious taste and aroma. And it's very hot! Look for bright peppers with no blemishes. To make the chilli less spicy, remove the seeds and inner ribs before cooking and make sure you wash your hands after handling them.

SNAPPER One of our most favoured types of fish, with its firm flesh and great taste.

SPRING ONIONS Known in the Caribbean as 'scallions'. Milder in taste compared to onions, these are much used in our food and make up part of the classic jerk seasoning.

SWEET POTATO More commonly used in Jamaica than the usual potatoes, which are called 'Irish Potatoes' there. Used in soups and curries. Sweet potatoes in Jamaica tend to be yellow inside whereas orange is more common in the UK.

THYME An important herb for Caribbean cooking, this gives a great flavour to many dishes. Sold in bunches of fresh or dried sprigs.

TUBERS AND ROOT VEGETABLES Hearty and nutritious vegetables such as cassava, dasheen (taro), eddoes, sweet potatoes and yams, most commonly used in soups and also boiled to be eaten as hard food.

TURMERIC Ground turmeric adds a strong yellow colour and flavour to food, including currries and patties. Caution: turmeric will stain white and lightly coloured clothes, as well as your hands, chopping boards and work surfaces.

YAMS Peeled and then usually steamed or boiled to make a filling carbohydrate that is served as part of our hard food. We like the yellow yam best for da' flava.

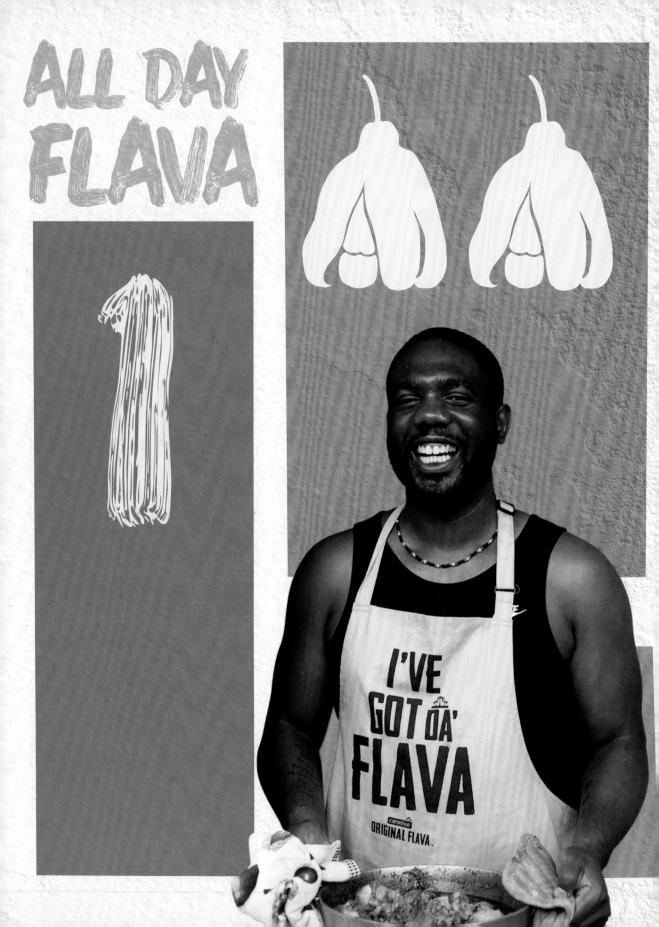

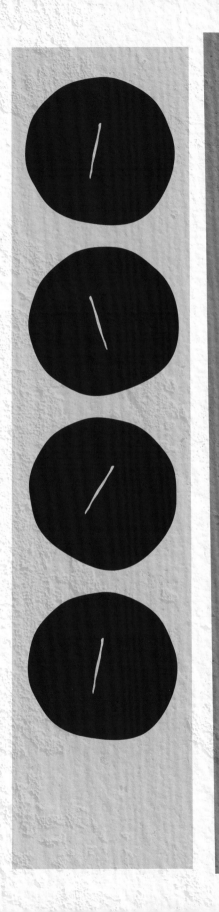

We always liked waking up to the sweet smell of breakfast – and still do! In Jamaica, people often eat a big meal in the marnin' to keep them going through the day, and that's why we have so many versatile and enjoyable dishes that are eaten for breakfast, brunch, lunch or dinner. Here are some of our most-loved foods, such as Ackee and Saltfish and Mackerel Rundown – and who can forget Fried Dumplings? One of our all-time favourites and good to eat at any time of day, and any day! All of these will be sure to bring da' sunshine to your meals, night or day.

ACKEE AND SALTFISH

Jamaica's national dish and one of our faves. Eat with some fried dumpling pon di side – **JEEZ!** Our love for ackee and saltfish started at a young age when our mum made it every Christmas morning; we looked forward to it more than the presents! Traditionally this is for the morning, but is so versatile you can eat it any time of the day. Ackee – which has a texture similar to scrambled eggs – is available in UK shops in cans, but in the Caribbean the fruit is picked fresh from the trees. You have to be careful to pick it when it is properly ripe because otherwise it can be poisonous. But be not afraid, the canned ones are perfectly safe! In this dish it's married with boneless saltfish flava'd up with ground Caribbean spices.

SERVES 4-6

- 600g boneless saltfish cod
- 2 tbsp vegetable oil
- 1 medium onion, finely diced
- 4 garlic cloves, finely chopped
- 3 spring onions, thinly sliced
- 1 scotch bonnet pepper, deseeded and finely chopped
- 1 tsp dried thyme
- 1 tsp ground pimento (allspice)
- ½ red bell pepper, deseeded and finely diced
- ½ green bell pepper, deseeded and finely diced
- 1 large tomato, diced
- 2 x 540g cans ackee, drained
- Freshly ground black pepper

Put the saltfish in your pot and cover with cold water. Bring to the boil, then boil for 5 minutes, drain and add fresh cold water to cover. Repeat this process until you're happy with the saltiness when tasted; we boil the fish three times in total for a perfect balance of salt in the fish. Drain for the final time and leave to cool. Use a fork to shred the saltfish into pieces and set aside.

Now you'll need a large frying pan. Pour the vegetable oil into the frying pan and place over a high heat. Once the oil is sizzling hot, turn the heat down to low-medium. Add the onion, garlic, spring onions and scotch bonnet, then cook until soft, for around 5-7 minutes.

Add the saltfish, dash in some black pepper, the thyme and pimento or allspice, then mix di ting together and cook down for around 3 minutes.

Next, add in the red and green bell peppers, along with your tomato. Mix together and cook down for 2-3 minutes. These ingredients help to bring a heat balance, so it's not too spicy.

Now you'll need to add in your ackee and dash in a likkle more black pepper. Fold in the ackee; the ackee is soft so it's important to fold it in very gently – nobody likes mushy ackee. Once folded in, simmer for 3-5 minutes before serving. Food **DUN!** Enjoy.

BRIT-CARIBBEAN BREAKFAST BOWL

We call this the Half British/Half Caribbean. Growing up in London in a Caribbean family means we enjoy the best of both worlds. After a long night, we have your typical morning fry-up, but Mum always throws in some Caribbean **FLAVA**, with the ackee and dumplings!

SERVES 4

8 vegan sausages

Olive oil, for cooking

4 tomatoes, halved

125g mushrooms, sliced

1 x 400g can baked beans

Vegetable oil, for frying

1 plantain, sliced into lengths

1 avocado, stoned and sliced

Salt, freshly ground black pepper, dried thyme and paprika, to taste

FOR THE DUMPLINGS

250g self-raising flour

1 tsp each of salt, brown sugar and vegan butter

Vegetable oil, for frying

FOR THE ACKEE

1 medium onion, diced

2 garlic cloves, finely chopped

1 small tomato, chopped

¼ red bell pepper, diced

¼ green bell pepper, diced

1 scotch bonnet pepper, diced

1 x 540g can ackee, drained

2 tsp freshly ground black pepper

4 fresh thyme sprigs

1 tsp paprika

Preheat the oven to 160°C Fan/180°C/Gas 4. Place the vegan sausages on a baking tray and cook in the centre of the oven for 15 minutes.

Meanwhile, make the dumplings. Combine the flour, salt and sugar in a bowl, then rub in the butter. Gradually add 120ml cold water. Knead to form a dough, then roll into a ball and let sit for 10 minutes.

For the ackee, heat 1 tbsp olive oil in a pan over a medium heat. Add the onion, garlic, tomato, bell peppers and scotch bonnet and sauté for 5–7 minutes until soft. Fold the ackee through with the pepper, thyme and paprika. Cook over a low heat for 5 minutes.

Place the tomatoes on a baking tray and sprinkle with salt. Cook under a hot grill for 15 minutes. Heat 1 tbsp olive oil in a frying pan over a high heat. Add the mushrooms, then add salt, pepper, thyme and paprika to taste. Cook for 10 minutes. Gently warm the beans in a pan for 5 minutes with paprika and pepper to taste.

Heat enough vegetable oil in a pan to shallow-fry, add the plantain slices and cook until golden on each side.

Take a golfball-sized piece of dumpling dough (about 50g), and roll it into a neat ball. Press down in the middle to make a deep indent. Heat a frying pan with enough vegetable oil to shallow-fry over a high heat. Add the dumplings and reduce the heat to medium. Cook for 3–4 minutes on each side until golden.

Plate everything up and top with some sliced avocado.

MACKEREL RUNDOWN

This is our nan's favourite dish: mackerel cooked in a coconut-enriched, spicy and creamy curry sauce. The blend of coconut and scotch bonnet combined with the mackerel produces an iconic taste favoured by many Caribbeans.

Nan actually uses canned mackerel these days for convenience, especially if she's not able to go to the shops. Either way, she often eats it with hard food - in this case, boiled dumpling and green banana, scooping them into the curry and eating everything together.

It's a really easy dish - around 20 minutes - and affordable too, plus you've got the flexibility of using canned mackerel or fresh. All of this makes it great for the family or something to make up quickly for dinner.

SERVES 4-6

1 x 400ml can coconut milk

1 tbsp curry powder

1 medium onion, diced

¼ red bell pepper, sliced

¼ green bell pepper, sliced

¼ yellow bell pepper, sliced

4 garlic cloves, chopped

1 tomato, diced

3 spring onions, sliced

1 scotch bonnet pepper, deseeded and diced

1 tsp fish seasoning

1 tsp freshly ground black pepper

1 tsp dried thyme

1 tsp paprika

1 x 400g can mackerel, drained and flaked, or 400g fresh fillets, cut into 5-7cm pieces

Pour the coconut milk into a saucepan and bring to the boil over a medium-high heat. Stir until it reduces to a thick, curded consistency.

Add the curry powder, onion, bell peppers, garlic, tomato, spring onions and scotch bonnet, then add the fish seasoning, black pepper, thyme and paprika. Stir and cook down over a medium heat until the onion is soft.

If using fresh mackerel, add it to the pan skin-side down and mix together with the sauce. Reduce to a low heat and simmer for about 10 minutes, or until the fish is cooked. If using canned mackerel, add to the sauce and cook for 2-3 minutes, or until heated through.

EAT WITH Hard food (see page 23) or Cook-Down Ackee and Callaloo (see page 142).

SALTFISH FRITTERS

The sight and smell of these crunchy fritters always excites us – they are so good and comforting to eat. We used to run downstairs for breakfast at Nan's when we woke up and smelled them cooking, and now it's always a happy feeling seeing these bad boys on the table.

In Jamaica, this is a traditional dish for the morning, and is nicknamed 'stamp 'n' go' as it's quick to make and you'd give it to the family as they went on their way to school or work. But we nyam them all day, every day, and one of our favourite ways to eat them is sandwiched between some hard dough bread, just like Auntie Eloise gave us when we visited her in Jamaica. She makes incredible saltfish fritters and I'm sure she'd be proud of our recipe, too.

SERVES 6

350g boneless saltfish cod

1 tsp baking powder

1 medium onion, diced

1 scotch bonnet pepper, deseeded and diced

1 tsp chilli powder or hot pepper sauce, to your taste

1 tbsp all-purpose seasoning

1 tsp freshly ground black pepper

2 garlic cloves, finely chopped

2 tsp dried thyme

3 spring onions, sliced

¼ green bell pepper, diced

¼ red bell pepper, diced

2 small tomatoes, diced

300g plain flour

Vegetable oil, for shallow-frying

Salt

TO SERVE

Sweet chilli sauce

Thinly sliced spring onions

Thinly sliced chilli

Put the saltfish in your pot and cover with cold water. Bring to the boil, then boil for 5 minutes, drain and add fresh cold water to cover. Repeat this process until you're happy with the saltiness when you taste it; we tend to boil the fish three times in total to leave a perfect balance of salt in the fish. Drain for the final time and set aside until cool enough to handle.

Use a fork or your hands to shred the saltfish into small pieces, then put it into a mixing bowl. Add the baking powder, onion, scotch bonnet, chilli powder or hot pepper sauce, all-purpose seasoning, black pepper, garlic, thyme, spring onions, bell peppers and tomatoes to the bowl, then add 250ml cold water.

Add the flour and mix everything together. The mixture should be a thick, sloppy consistency – add more flour or water as necessary.

Pour enough oil into a frying pan to half-fill it and place over a high heat. Once the oil is piping hot, turn down to a medium–high heat. Use a large spoon to scoop spoonfuls of the mixture into the pan and cook until golden and crispy, around 3–4 minutes on each side. Drain on kitchen paper and sprinkle with a likkle salt before serving with sweet chilli sauce for dipping, and sliced spring onion and chilli sprinkled over to garnish.

PLANTAIN FOUR WAYS

We love plantain so much for its versatility, and have fun cooking it in different ways – here are four super-easy suggestions for being creative with it. This naturally sweet and tasty Jamaican staple can accompany a range of dishes, or just be eaten as it is.

There are traditional ways of cutting plantain. For frying, you usually cut it in a medium-to-long slant. We love to create plantain fries with a crunchy coating, either fried or oven-baked and eaten with a chilli dip to flava them up a bit.

SERVES 4 AS A SIDE

2 plantain

Vegetable oil, for shallow- or deep-frying

Salt

FOR THE PLANTAIN FRIES

2 tbsp plain flour

1 tsp cornflour

75ml coconut milk

To prepare the plantain, use a sharp knife to cut off both tip ends of each plantain and then gently score a line along the full length, making sure you don't cut the inside flesh. Remove the skin by peeling from the score line.

Traditional (top left) Cut the plantain in half across the middle. Take one half, then slice lengthways from the cut end down to the tip. You should be able to get about three slices from each half.

Sliced (bottom left) Nice and easy. Cut the plantain crossways into circles about 1cm thick.

Slanted (bottom right) Cut the plantain on a diagonal into slanted slices about 2cm thick.

Fries (centre) Cut the plantain in half lengthways, then cut each long piece in half. Cut these pieces lengthways into chips.

continued overleaf

To cook the traditional, slanted and sliced plantain: put enough oil into a frying pan for shallow-frying and place over a medium heat. Once hot, add the plantain, working in batches so you don't overcrowd the pan. Cook the traditional and sliced for 1–2 minutes on each side, or until golden, and the slanted for 2 minutes on each side, keeping an eye on them to make sure they do not catch. Remove from the oil, drain on kitchen paper and sprinkle with salt.

To cook the fries: put the plantain fries into a mixing bowl, dash in the plain flour, cornflour and coconut milk, then mix together. Heat the oil in a frying pan until piping hot, then turn down to medium-high and carefully add the fries in batches to the hot oil, one by one. Cook each batch for about 2 minutes on each side, so about 8 minutes in total, then drain on kitchen paper and sprinkle with a likkle salt.

 Nuff tings – with your Ackee and Saltfish (see page 29), Rice and Peas (see page 59), and Jerk Chicken (see page 105). It's a versatile dish!

 Slice the plantain into rounds 1cm thick, spread out on a baking tray, drizzle with oil and sprinkle with salt then bake in an oven preheated to 160°C Fan/180°C/ Gas 4 for 30 minutes. Serve them as an alternative to potato crisps.

FRIED DUMPLINGS

Indulgent and highly addictive, these fried dumplings are a staple of the Caribbean plate – warm and crunchy, yet soft in the middle. They're also one of our favourite things to eat all day, every day, with everything. We can't believe how such a tasty dish can be so simple – made from just four main ingredients: flour, sugar, salt and water (plus oil for frying). You can add other ingredients, such as butter and cornmeal, but – trust us – it's as good with just the Fantastic Four.

One trick to making dumplings is to know that they get better with confidence and practice. Be in control of the dough while kneading – don't let the dough control you. There are multiple ways to create a perfect dumpling shape and everyone insists that their dumplings are the best, not just in taste, but looks as well. What you do is completely up to you. Nan always says just go with how you feel – or what's comfortable!

SERVES 4

| 500g self-raising flour |
| A likkle bit of sugar |
| A likkle bit of salt |
| 1 tsp butter (optional) |
| 200–250ml water |
| Vegetable oil, for shallow-frying |

To make the dough, put the flour into a bowl, add the sugar and salt, then mix together with your hands or a spoon. Rub in the butter, if using. Add the water a small amount at a time, kneading it in with your hands, until you have a large ball of dough. It'll be a bit sticky at first, but after kneading for a couple of minutes the dough should be soft and should not stick to your hands (if your dough is too dry, add a likkle more water and knead it into the dough; if too wet, dash in some flour).

To shape your dumplings, tear off a golfball-sized piece of dough and place it in the palm of one hand. Then move the dough around in a circular motion with your other palm. Once a ball shape is created, gently press the ball down, and with your thumb press a dimple in the centre of the dumpling.

Pour enough oil for shallow-frying into a frying pan and place over a high heat. Once hot, turn down to medium–high, so you don't burn up the dumplings. Then, in batches so you don't overcrowd the pan, add the dumplings carefully to the hot oil and fry for a few minutes until golden brown on the first side. Prick them with a fork to help the heat get to the centre of the dumplings, then turn and cook for a few more minutes until golden all over. Drain the fried dumplings on kitchen paper to soak up the excess oil.

SCHOOL FOOD

On our journey to Jamaica, we went to spend a day in Moreland Hill Primary School, up in the hills in Westmoreland in the southwest. There were echoes of Nan's childhood – some of the kids walk a long way to get to school, just like she did back in the day.

These schoolkids might not have much in material terms but they were so happy and glad to see us. They were very respectful, saying *'Welcome, good morning!'* together in harmony, and wearing uniform, with the girls matching their hair beads to their clothes. The teachers were very affectionate and the kids full of life. And there was a lot of food knowledge from a young age – when they saw a photograph of one of our dishes, Mackerel Rundown, they knew it was canned fish and not fresh.

We made plantain fritters as a cooking lesson, just like when we were young and saw Nanny and Mum make fritters and then did it ourselves – that's how you learn. Their school dinner looked GOOD: brown stew chicken and white rice. And then they wanted to know everything about us *'What do you do? Do you play football?'* Which

led to them pulling us by our shirts to play football with them outside. They were so strong in the tackle – must be all that hard food!

Back home in Britain, we do workshops at schools to inspire kids to cook. They find our lessons and online cooking interesting because it may well be food they recognise and enjoy. Rather than buying greasy chicken and chips, they are fascinated to see the whole process of making fresh food and think *'I want to do this, I can do this.'*

The schools we visit are usually in areas that are statistically quite bad for crime. Even at our school growing up, people were involved in the gang culture. But if you get kids disciplined and inspired, it helps them when they get older. It makes a difference that we can relate to their experiences, and the

challenges of growing up in the kind of society we're in now.

So many aspects and attributes of cooking can benefit a young person. Food is a common ground that people of all ages relate to. For some, it can be a way of escaping from a troublesome home, as they might excel in food when they're not into other parts of the curriculum, or think about making it into a business. Caribbean kids can grow up not knowing how to make their own food. For others, we show them how to make easy, authentic recipes from another culture.

Celebrity chefs are often far-fetched with their recipes, with no connection to the everyday person. If kids know and like a dish, and can make it themselves, it gives them a sense of achievement and helps their confidence and self-esteem, team-building, and even family-building. People don't understand how food can change lives. If you don't grow up with good food, you don't realise what a difference it can make. But it should be part of education, just like maths and English. Kids are the future – and we think cooking's the future too.

CORNMEAL PORRIDGE

Sweet, thick and filling, porridge gives you a warming feeling. For us it holds so many memories of when we were growing up and staying round at Nan's house. She gave it to us on those cold winter mornings, and every warm spoonful would rest so delightfully on our tastebuds.

The rich flavour of the cornmeal, nutmeg and sweetened condensed milk hits you from the first mouthful and makes this such an enjoyable breakfast dish, but also one of those dishes that you look forward to before you go to bed – a comfort food at any time.

We always add sugar according to however we feel on that day: if we need more comforting, then more sugar! But we remember pouring in the sugar as kids, and Nan slapping our hands, saying 'Not too much!' For an alternative sweetener, add fruit such as mango or blueberries.

SERVES 2

300g fine cornmeal

250ml whole milk

750ml water

1 tsp ground cinnamon or ½ cinnamon stick

2 tbsp sweetened condensed milk, or to taste

1 tsp freshly grated nutmeg, to taste

A likkle bit of salt

1 tsp vanilla extract

A likkle bit of sugar, to taste, or fresh fruit, such as mango slices or blueberries

A likkle bit of ground cinnamon, to serve

Combine the cornmeal and milk in a mixing bowl. Pour the water into a saucepan and bring to the boil over a high heat. Add the cornmeal mixture and stir until it thickens, then turn down to a low–medium heat once it begins to bubble.

Add the cinnamon, sweetened condensed milk, nutmeg, salt and vanilla and give it a good stir.

Reduce to a low heat and let the porridge simmer for 15 minutes, stirring constantly, until fully cooked and nicely thickened. Allow to cool down slightly before serving. Add sugar or fresh fruit to your preferred taste, then sprinkle over a likkle extra cinnamon.

 Some people dip pieces of hard-dough bread into their porridge, or add banana as a topping.

 Use dairy-free products like almond or soya milk instead of whole milk and sweetened condensed milk.

 If you want a lighter option, add more cinnamon and nutmeg and less sugar.

PEANUT, GREEN BANANA AND OATMEAL PORRIDGES

Porridge is one of the most common breakfasts in the Caribbean. Because Jamaica is such a hot country, some may find that bizarre. But when you taste the different porridges available in Jamaica, you'll understand why! Also, making porridge is easy and adaptable and it doesn't cost much to make huge quantities, which is perfect if you have a big family. It used to be traditional in families to have between six and ten children, so porridge was a great and inexpensive way to make sure they were 'belly full' for the majority of the day. Cooks found different flavour options to give a twist to this practical gem and they've been passed down the generations.

Cornmeal porridge is the most popular porridge in today's Caribbean community, but others, such as peanut, oatmeal and green banana come a close second. We want to bring back all the original **FLAVAS!**

PEANUT PORRIDGE

SERVES 2

250g raw peanuts
250ml coconut milk
250ml whole milk
125ml water
1 tsp vanilla extract
125ml sweetened condensed milk
1 tsp ground cinnamon or freshly grated nutmeg
1 tsp salt

First, rinse the peanuts in water and soak for a few hours in plenty of cold water.

Drain the soaked nuts and add to a blender with the coconut milk and whole milk. Blend for 3–5 minutes until finely ground.

Bring the water to the boil in a saucepan, then add the peanut mixture and stir together to mix. Add the vanilla extract, condensed milk, cinnamon or nutmeg and salt. Stir until the mixture thickens.

Continue to simmer for 15 minutes over a low-medium heat, stirring regularly.

GREEN BANANA PORRIDGE

SERVES 2

2 green (unripe) bananas

250ml water

250ml coconut milk

125ml sweetened condensed milk

1 tsp vanilla extract

½ tsp ground cinnamon

½ tsp freshly grated nutmeg

½ tsp salt

Cut the ends off each banana, then score down the middle and peel off the skin.

Add the bananas to a blender with the water and coconut milk and blend for 5 minutes. Transfer the mixture to a saucepan, bring to the boil and add the condensed milk, vanilla extract, cinnamon, nutmeg and salt and stir well.

Cook for 15 minutes, stirring over a low-medium heat, until thickened.

OATMEAL PORRIDGE

SERVES 2

600ml almond milk or whole milk

100g porridge oats

1 tsp vanilla extract

1 tsp freshly grated nutmeg

1 tsp ground cinnamon

1 tsp salt

2 tbsp sugar

Firstly pour the milk into a saucepan and bring to the boil. Then add the oats and stir well until thick.

Add the vanilla extract, nutmeg, cinnamon, salt and sugar and whisk together.

Continue to cook for 15 minutes over a low-medium heat, stirring, until cooked and nicely thickened.

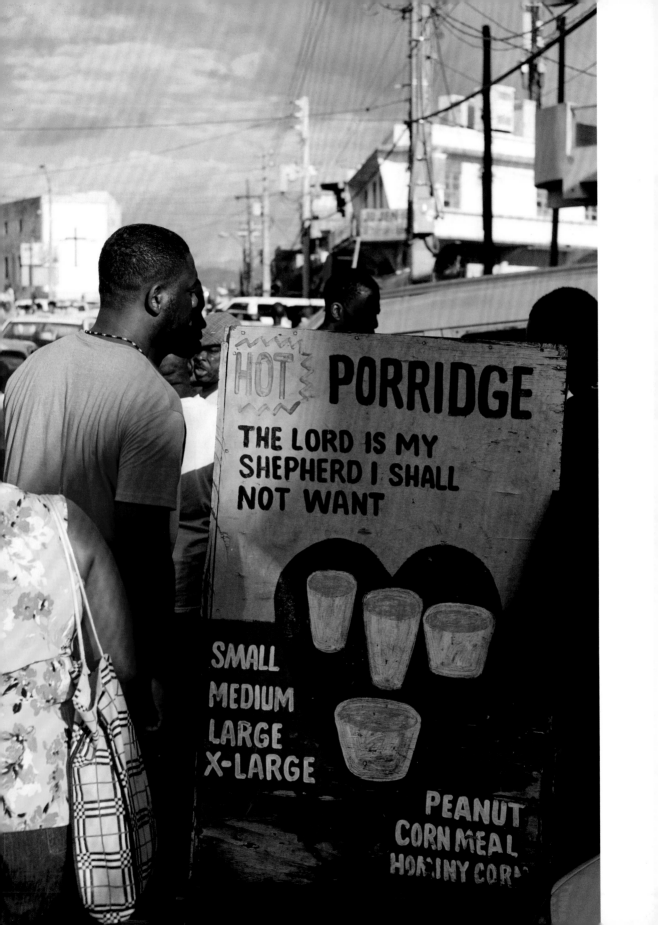

ITAL JUICE

This smoothie is full of life. Our nan grows aloe vera in her garden and all over the house, too. Our mum cuts off pieces of aloe leaf with scissors to use in hair oil or body lotion. An aspiring nutritionist, she uses natural ingredients in food and started using it in her smoothies. So we had to add aloe vera to our green juice, which is full of energy-boosting ingredients that get you ready for the day ahead. You'll be a lean, green machine once you gulp this one down – **AWOAH!**

SERVES 2

1 cucumber, peeled and chopped

1 tbsp aloe vera leaf gel (scooped out of a cut leaf) or aloe vera juice

½ tsp ground ginger

1 apple, quartered and sliced

Handful of callaloo (or spinach)

Juice of ½ lime

250ml coconut water

Put all the ingredients into a blender and blend together to create a thick smoothie. Strain through a sieve and serve.

RISE 'N' SHINE MANGO SMOOTHIE

The taste of the Caribbean, all in one smoothie! Mango is one of the most popular fruits in Jamaica and we picked some fresh and juicy ones from our uncle's tree in Clarendon. Make sure your fruit is really ripe before you make this delicious drink.

SERVES 2

1 medium-sized ripe mango, peeled and cubed

5 ice cubes

2 passionfruit, halved and flesh scooped out, or 200ml passionfruit juice

½ medium banana

250ml coconut water

Put all the ingredients into a blender and blend together. Strain through a sieve and serve.

TOP 10 THINGS #GROWINGUPCARIBBEAN

Who can forget what it was like growing up in a Caribbean home? Alongside fearing your parents over anything to do with school, food, chores and ornaments were the major features of our lives – to name a few!

Although we can't rewind the clock, we thought we'd reminisce on 10 THINGS we experienced growing up.

1. You had to clean every Saturday morning
Lie-ins didn't exist. And you could forget about watching cartoons too. The house had to be cleaned from top to bottom and the clothes had to be ironed for church the next day or school the following week – and there was no escaping it. Sometimes, it would even run into the afternoon when you had plans. You just had to suck it up and clean without looking miserable.

2. Waking up to the smell of food The weekend hadn't started unless the smell of something amazing woke you up with a smile. It didn't matter what it was; it smelt great. If you were really lucky it was a full-on breakfast of Ackee and Saltfish with Fried Dumplings or Mackerel Rundown with boiled green banana and dumplings. These dishes would keep you satisfied for most of the day.

3. Singing while cooking = a feast for dinner
The chef of the house would either hum or sing when they cooked. That was a sign that it was about to go down in the kitchen. Once the singing began, the smell of food filled the house. On the odd occasion, though, the sweet-smelling food was for someone else...

4. Sneaking in the kitchen to eat from the Dutch pot (quietly) Yes. We all did it, even though we were strictly told not to touch the pot until it was dinner time. We couldn't help ourselves. It was the same routine every week: you ran to get a fork or spoon, tip-toed back to the pot and helped yourself to whatever was inside.

5. Getting told off for eating from the pot when your mum's in the other room Seriously, though, how did she hear us? We were extra careful when taking the closest piece of meat. Yet despite our careful planning and silence, she just knew what we were about to do and shouted at us even though she couldn't see us. It's scary.

6. Three carbs in one meal was standard You weren't really hungry but you couldn't resist the food. Rice and Peas took up most of the plate, then Mac 'n' Cheese and then roast potatoes with meat and (overcooked) veg. You tackled the feast and then you hated yourself because you couldn't move. Then an hour later (yeah right, 30 minutes max), you helped yourself to seconds as if you hadn't learnt anything the first time around.

7. You couldn't use any of the stuff in the cabinet
You'll never forget the 'good' crockery and glasses that only surfaced once a year, twice if you were lucky. In fact, they're probably still there now. And don't get us started on the plates with the gold rim that couldn't go in the microwave... Don't take the plastic slipcovers off the couch – even though it's more than 20 years old!

8. What was up with the plastic covers? They were awkward to sit on and it made getting comfortable a longer process than necessary. It was either freezing to sit on in winter or unbearable when it's hot and sticky in summer. But... rules were rules and you had to obey.

9. The living room was only for special guests
The living room was almost always locked and you never knew where the key was. But when the doorbell rang, your parents ushered guests into the living room. And you, sadly, weren't invited to join. You had to know your place.

10. The ice-cream container that never had ice cream in it! You 100% wanted the Neapolitan ice cream but instead you got leftovers from some time or another. And then you lost hope of there ever being real ice cream in the freezer. The disappointment was real! Word of warning: don't trust the ice-cream tub.

Our parents used to say, it takes a whole village to raise a child; we say it takes a good side to complete a delicious meal! Caribbean food is known for its flavalicious sides. These ones perfectly complement our mains and many are just as great on their own. Seasoned-up rice is a speciality, from the classic Rice and Peas to spiced Pumpkin Rice and other delicious kinds that we've shared here. Then there's hard food, a staple inclusion in an authentic Jamaican meal that's a mix of nutritious starchy foods to soak up tasty sauces and provide incredible nutritional benefits to help make you strong – just like the Jamaican locals say. There's our own spin on Mac 'n' Cheese, our signature Coleslaw and an easy home-cooked version of the classic Trinidadian Roti flatbread. We've also given some of our favourite sauces to eat pon di side, including a hot, hot, HOT scotch bonnet sauce, and others too. Ya mon, da ting set good!

RICE AND PEAS

An iconic Jamaican dish, this is full of amazing spices and seasoned to perfection. The cooking method is an expression of love. Take time to give your food TLC and you'll see the improvement in taste! In Caribbean homes, especially on Sundays, people cook from early morning to make sure dishes are just right. They understand that with great food comes great memories. We call it 'Rice and Peas', but in fact we mostly use kidney beans, or gungo (pigeon) peas. We boil up dried peas for a richer colour, but they can take an hour to soften. A trick we've learned, when short on time, is to use canned instead and add ½ tsp browning for that rich colour.

SERVES 4-5

200g dried red kidney beans or gungo peas or 1 x 400g can gungo peas or red kidney beans

1 tsp salt

1 tsp freshly ground black pepper

1 medium onion, finely chopped

2 spring onions, sliced in half lengthways

Handful of fresh thyme sprigs

4 garlic cloves, finely chopped

2 tbsp all-purpose seasoning

½ tsp browning or dark soy sauce (if using canned peas; see introduction)

100g creamed coconut, broken into pieces, or 1 x 400ml can coconut milk

600g long-grain or basmati rice

1 tsp pimento (allspice) berries

1 scotch bonnet pepper

If using dried red kidney beans or gungo peas, rinse well and tip into a large pot. Pour in enough water to cover the peas by 10cm. If you have time, soak the peas overnight; this gives a richer colour. Alternatively, skip this step and go straight to boiling the peas. If using canned peas, empty the cans, including the liquid, into the pot and add water to cover the peas by 10cm.

Bring to the boil then add the salt, pepper, onion, spring onions, thyme, garlic, all-purpose seasoning, browning or soy (if using canned peas) and creamed coconut or coconut milk. Simmer over a medium–high heat for 1½ hours until soft if using unsoaked dried peas, or 1 hour if soaked, adding more water as necessary. If using canned, simmer for just 10 minutes.

Rinse the rice under cold running water and add to your pot. Make sure the level of the liquid is slightly above the rice. Mix together then add the pimento or allspice and scotch bonnet - this gives a spicy kick - and cover with a lid. Cook for 20 minutes over a low heat, giving it a stir halfway through the cooking time and checking now and then to make sure the rice isn't catching on the bottom of the pot. Add a likkle water if necessary.

Once the rice is cooked, take off the heat, remove and discard the scotch bonnet, spring onions and thyme. Mix the rice in from the bottom, place the lid back on and leave to steam for 15 minutes until fluffy.

PELAU – ONE-POT CHICKEN AND RICE

Known as one of Trinidad's most loved dishes, this is a fusion of flavours that creates an easy one-pot dish for everyone to enjoy. A mixture of vegetables, with spices infused into the rice and chicken pieces, this dish is also similar to Guyanese cook-up, but is inspired by an African tradition of cooking everything in one pot. Easy recipe – and not much washing-up to do either!

SERVES 4–6

750g bone-in chicken pieces, skin removed

4 tbsp Green Seasoning (see page 86)

1 tsp salt

1 tbsp tomato ketchup

1 tbsp dark soy sauce or browning

1 tbsp olive oil or coconut oil

1 tbsp brown sugar

1 medium onion, diced

4 garlic cloves, finely chopped

350g long-grain brown rice, rinsed

1 x 400g can green pigeon peas, drained and rinsed

1 x 400ml can coconut milk

1 celery stick, finely chopped

250g butternut squash, peeled, deseeded and chopped into 3.5cm chunks (optional)

1 large carrot, diced

2–3 fresh thyme sprigs

1 tbsp turmeric

1 tsp freshly ground black pepper

1 scotch bonnet pepper

1–2 tbsp butter

Season the chicken pieces all over with 3 tbsp of the green seasoning, the salt, ketchup and soy sauce or browning. Mix up di ting, cover and marinate for at least 1 hour or overnight in the fridge.

Put the oil into a large shallow pan and place over a medium heat. Once hot, add the sugar and let it melt, stirring constantly. When the sugar and oil turn slightly frothy and liquid, add the onion and garlic and sizzle for a couple of minutes, then dash in the seasoned chicken and mix it up until it is coated all over. Cook for around 2 minutes.

Add the rice and pigeon peas and mix together, then fling in the coconut milk and 125ml cold water. Mix together and level the ingredients so the liquid is at least double the volume of the rice (add a little more water if not). Add the celery, squash (if using), carrot, thyme sprigs, turmeric, black pepper and the remaining 1 tbsp green seasoning and mix around. Place the scotch bonnet in the rice and bring to the boil. Cover, reduce the heat to low and simmer for about 30 minutes until the liquid is absorbed and the rice is cooked.

If you want the rice slightly more wet, add more water. Add the butter and mix everything together. **<u>JEEZ!</u>** Enjoy the da' flava!

PUMPKIN RICE

This recipe is full of flavaful spices to give the dish a mild kick and a warm, scented aroma, and its authentic, rich colour comes from adding pumpkin. All in all, it's an exciting way to spice up ya rice! The recipe is straight from Jamaica, where we had it for the first time in our family's homes and also from street-food stalls.

The pumpkin season is short, but you can use butternut squash as an alternative. Why not try it with some tasty roasted veg skewers or curry chicken? The flavours will give you that Caribbean spicy feeling. **YA MON!**

SERVES 4

1 tbsp olive oil

1 small onion, diced

1 small red onion, diced

4 garlic cloves, finely chopped

1 tsp salt

1 tsp freshly ground black pepper

1 tsp ground pimento (allspice)

Handful of fresh thyme sprigs

500g pumpkin or butternut squash, peeled, deseeded and diced

250ml vegetable stock

250ml coconut milk

1 scotch bonnet pepper

400g long-grain or basmati rice

Add the oil to a large pot over a high heat, then add the onions and garlic. Cook down over a medium heat for 5–7 minutes until soft.

Season with the salt, black pepper, pimento and thyme, then add the diced pumpkin or squash and mix together. Add 250ml cold water, bring to the boil and simmer for 15 minutes. Add the stock and coconut milk, along with the scotch bonnet.

Rinse the rice well under cold running water, then add to the pot. Cook for 15 minutes, stirring from time to time, until the rice is cooked. Season to taste and serve.

SPICY FLAVA

Jamaican food is an adventure for the palate and the flava's got to be STRONG. You have to *feel* the taste. A lot of that comes from the spices and mixtures that bring the unique flava so many people enjoy. Salt and pepper are not enough for us!

The taste of spice is the taste of home. One of our early food memories was our grandad's breakfasts when we stayed with Nanny McAnuff in the summer holidays. He didn't cook that much, so in the mornings he'd give us tea and thick, thick, unevenly cut slices of Bulla Bread, warmed up and spread with butter. It's real old-school, deep spice: a lot of ginger, cinnamon and mixed spice – the taste's similar to Bun, another classic Jamaican bake.

We were always taught to use a combination of different spices to create a meal – *'use whatever unuh have in the cupboard.'* It was especially important to marinate the meat in spices overnight for the best taste ever, and we'd watch our mum and grandma preparing food the night before as part of

the process of cooking. Often their food included spring onions (called scallions in Jamaica), scotch bonnet pepper, pimento and thyme, and this combination is famously known as the jerk flava that's used for chicken on the grill.

Go to a Caribbean kitchen and you'll see the same pots of spice. One that connects to Britain is ginger. Jamaican ginger is famous for its quality and heat and it's used a lot, either grated or as a powder, both to give a dish more kick and to balance the other flavours. Ginger cake and ginger beer are two Jamaican classics known everywhere in the UK, but ginger is also essential in our Christmas sorrel drink. Pimento is also a must-have spice – both the whole berries and ground up. It's known in Britain as allspice because it captures the fragrance of different spices.

We've got some spice mixes too. For an Indian curry, the spices are added separately but Jamaican curry powder is a ready-made mix that goes into Curry Chicken, Curry Goat – Curry EVERYTING! There's also all-purpose seasoning, which is a mix of typical Jamaican spices. We use it in some recipes in this book, but have mostly put our own blend of different spices in the pot.

On our first day in Jamaica, we went to the market in Montego Bay and there were tablefuls of big bags of spices, not just little pots on a shelf. We'd never seen fresh nutmeg before, still with its lacy covering of mace. You can grate the nut into cornmeal porridge or infuse your mixture with just the shell.

We saw fields full of scotch bonnet peppers, with women picking them by hand in the blazing midday sun. They're sold on

big tables in the market stalls, the colours mixed together: gold, green, red – and even brown. People have preferences. We often go for red, because of the vivid colour; some people think yellow is the hottest and others insist on using only green in their spicy marinades.

Chillies, for us, are about fragrance as much as heat. We've grown up on Caribbean food and never think of it as hot – we see it more as flavourful. Sure, some people put in lots of pepper but there's a way to cook with

scotch bonnet so that it lingers rather than burns. You put the whole one in the dish to infuse its flavour and some heat but don't leave it in for too long. If you cut up a red chilli finely it looks good in the food and you can use just one in a big bowl of food. When using scotch bonnets, you can take out the seeds and the membranes – they hold the fiercest fire. And if you're cooking for people you don't know, it's best to make the food less hot and put a bottle of hot pepper sauce on the table.

WHAT UNUH HAVE IN DI CUPBOARD

HONEY MAC 'N' CHEESE

Our stomachs growl when we think of this dish. Mac 'n' cheese is known worldwide but in the Caribbean we REALLY flava it up. At family parties, it's the first to go - you even see family members sneaking containers out to pack some away to take home. We add an extra spin with the inclusion of sweet honey. Season the cheese sauce with scotch bonnet, thyme and garlic, use three different types of cheese, and layer the cheeses in between rows of macaroni. Then coat the top with more cheese and bake to create a slight crust on the top to produce the most flavaful taste. We usually serve it as a side, alongside some chicken, rice and salad. So it's part of a hearty meal or great at a BBQ too. You've got to try this recipe and feel **DA' FLAVA!**

SERVES 6-8

1 tbsp vegetable oil

1 medium onion, finely diced

2 tsp salt

1kg dried macaroni

1 tbsp butter

2 tsp freshly ground black pepper

500ml evaporated or whole milk

2 eggs, beaten

100g plain flour

1 tsp mustard

1 tsp paprika

1 tsp honey, plus extra to taste

1 tsp chilli powder

1 scotch bonnet pepper, deseeded and diced

300g red Leicester cheese, grated

300g mild Cheddar, grated

300g mozzarella, grated

50g cream crackers, crushed into very fine crumbs (or use cheese crackers or Doritos)

Preheat the oven to 160°C Fan/180°C/Gas 4. Heat the vegetable oil in a pan over a medium heat, then add the onion and cook for 5 minutes, or until soft. Set aside.

Bring a large saucepan of water to the boil, add the salt and macaroni and cook for 10 minutes (do not fully cook as it will also go in the oven). Drain, return to the pan, add the butter and 1 tsp black pepper and mix well.

For the sauce, pour the milk into a bowl and add the eggs, flour, mustard, paprika, honey, chilli powder, remaining pepper, scotch bonnet and softened onion. Add 100g of each cheese to the mixture and whisk.

Pour the sauce onto the pasta and stir; this should give it a creamy, cheesy look. Get a large casserole dish and spoon in a layer of macaroni, about one third of the dish height, and then sprinkle with a third of the remaining cheeses. Add another layer of macaroni and sprinkle with more cheeses. Repeat these steps until you've used all the pasta, saving a good amount of cheese for the top layer.

Once the top layer is covered with cheeses, give it more added **FLAVA** by sprinkling over the cracker crumbs, then bake in the oven for 20-25 minutes until the inside is bubbling and the top is crispy. Once cooked, squeeze extra honey over to taste.

STEAMED CABBAGE

Shredded cabbage, colourful bell peppers and spring onions are stir-fried and then steamed with butter melted pon it to make a side dish that tastes as good as it looks. Often eaten with a main and some rice, this helps to create a great home-cooked meal and is seen as one of the most desirable sides at Caribbean restaurants around the world. Craig particularly enjoys it with some Escovitch Fish and Shaun enjoys it with Rice and Peas. Give it a go!

SERVES 4

1 tsp olive oil

2 tbsp butter

1 large white cabbage, cut into medium shreds

1 carrot, peeled and cut into thin strips

1 onion, halved and sliced

4 spring onions, cut into medium strips

¼ red bell pepper, cut into medium strips

1 x 165g can sweetcorn, drained

1 tsp salt

1 tsp freshly ground black pepper

Handful of fresh thyme sprigs

Put the olive oil and half the butter into a large frying pan to heat up. When hot, add the cabbage, carrot, onion, spring onions, bell pepper and sweetcorn. Mix together, put a lid on the pan and let the vegetables steam over a low heat for 10–12 minutes.

Season with the salt, black pepper and thyme and mix together.

Finally, add the remaining butter and let it melt into the vegetables to give them a nice shine.

COLESLAW

This is our Number One likkle side. Sunday dinner isn't complete without some crunchy coleslaw. However, it's a debate between us as to which style is the best. Shaun sides with Uncle Tim's crunchy coleslaw, with thicker cuts of veggies, against Auntie Janet's finely grated coleslaw – Craig's choice. Either way, Shaun's Christmas turns Grinch if he doesn't see coleslaw on the day. How you make it is totally up to you – let us know which you prefer!

SERVES 6–8

1 large white cabbage, outer leaves removed, shredded

2 carrots, grated

1 medium onion, finely diced

1 x 165g can sweetcorn, drained

½ red bell pepper, deseeded and diced

½ green bell pepper, deseeded and diced

½ scotch bonnet pepper, deseeded and finely diced

1 tbsp hot pepper sauce

1 x 340g jar mayonnaise

1 tbsp salad cream

1 tsp dried thyme

A likkle bit of salt

A likkle bit of freshly ground black pepper

1 tbsp honey (optional)

Mix your cabbage and carrots together in a large bowl. Add the onion, sweetcorn, bell pepper and scotch bonnet to the bowl.

Add the hot pepper sauce, mayonnaise, salad cream, dried thyme, salt, black pepper and honey (if using), and mix together well.

Crunchy coleslaw at its finest!

YAM MASH

Yam is one of the most commonly used root vegetables in the Caribbean, where it is often included in Sat'day soups, or boiled down and eaten as a side to curries, fish and meat dishes. Yams have a rough texture outside and a dense interior – in markets in Jamaica we saw strong women holding and peeling these humongous yams ready for people to cook.

This time we've put in some flavas and used a different process, making it into a mash, as a variation on potato. We add garlic, herbs and smoky paprika, and whip it up using crème fraîche, milk and butter. As yams have a sharper taste than potatoes, we'd encourage you to taste the mash as you go to check it's seasoned to your preference.

SERVES 6

2kg yam
Juice of 1 lime
4 tbsp softened butter
4 tbsp crème fraîche
200ml whole milk
1 tbsp dried mixed herbs
2 tbsp all-purpose seasoning
6 garlic cloves, crushed
2 tsp salt, or more to taste
2 tsp freshly ground black pepper
2 fresh thyme sprigs

Peel the yam using a sharp knife, then cut into 5cm cubes. Place the diced yam into a large bowl of cold water with the lime juice.

Get a big pan of water to boil your yam in and bring to the boil, adding a likkle bit of salt. Drain the diced yam from the lime water and add to the boiling water and boil until soft, around 20–25 minutes. Once soft, drain and mash up the yam with a potato masher.

Dash in the butter, a tablespoon at a time, mashing it down each time. This gives it an even spread of buttery goodness. Do the same with the crème fraîche, then pour in the milk and add the dried mixed herbs, all-purpose seasoning, garlic, salt, pepper and the thyme sprigs; these sprigs give the yam a fresh, scented aroma and taste.

Mash down all together until smooth, adding more milk to loosen if necessary. We like to use a fork to whisk at the end to give it that extra smoothness. Taste and adjust the seasoning to your preference.

GREEN BANANA POTATO SALAD

We saw this dish in Jamaica and loved the use of the green banana, which is often used in soups but this time is boiled and combined with potato to put a twist on the traditional family favourite of potato salad. We've flung in some diced veggies to add a tasty crunch and a mixture of seasonings to bring da' flava, whipped together with creamy mayonnaise.

An indulgent side dish, this is super-easy to make and works perfectly at a summer BBQ party. It's one of those dishes that will surprise your guests and have them coming back for seconds, saying **LAWD-AH-MERCY!**

SERVES 4

2 green (unripe) bananas

2 large white potatoes, washed, peeled and cut into 1cm dice (or use smaller salad potatoes, sliced)

1 small onion, chopped

1 small red onion, chopped

3 spring onions, sliced

½ red bell pepper, deseeded and diced

½ green bell pepper, deseeded and diced

1 x 165g can sweetcorn, drained

4 tbsp mayonnaise

1 tsp dried thyme

1 tsp salt

1 tsp freshly ground black pepper

First bring a large pan of salted water to the boil.

Cut the ends off your green bananas, then score a line down the middle of the skin and add (unpeeled) to your pan of boiling water. Cook for 20 minutes, or until soft. Using tongs, remove the bananas from the pan then carefully take the skin off and set aside to cool.

Cook the diced potato in the pan of boiling water for 5–10 minutes, or until tender, then drain and set aside to cool.

Cut the cooled bananas into slices and place in a large mixing bowl, along with the onions, spring onions, bell peppers, sweetcorn and drained potatoes and mix together. Add the mayo then season with the thyme, salt and black pepper. Gently mix again before serving.

CARIBBEAN BEAN SALAD

In Jamaica's markets, you'll often see stalls with a huge variety of home-grown beans to choose from. We were sold beans by the sweetest elderly lady in downtown Mobay Market, who knew every bean possible and told us the best for each dish. We were inspired by this great range to make a dish packed with the beans that are most often used in Caribbean dishes – butter beans, red kidney beans and black beans – tossed with vegetables, mixed herbs and an olive oil dressing to create a light but protein-packed salad.

We'd recommend serving this dish as a part of a lunch meal with friends or family, as it complements other dishes and creates a well-balanced feast. Using canned beans, it only takes 5 minutes or so to make and looks fantastic on the table.

**SERVES 6–8 AS A SIDE
OR 4 AS A MAIN**

1 x 400g can kidney beans, drained and rinsed

1 x 400g can black beans, drained and rinsed

1 x 400g can butter beans, drained and rinsed

1 small onion, diced

1 cucumber, diced

¼ red cabbage, sliced

½ white cabbage sliced

8 cherry tomatoes, quartered

50g fresh coriander or parsley, chopped

1 tsp dried thyme

1 tsp salt

1 tsp freshly ground black pepper

1 tbsp olive oil

60ml balsamic vinegar

Firstly, throw all the drained and rinsed beans into a large mixing bowl.

Add all the prepared vegetables, the coriander or parsley, and season with the thyme, salt and black pepper. Drizzle with the olive oil and add the balsamic vinegar, then toss di ting around with a large spoon.

CRUSTLESS CALLALOO QUICHE

Growing up, we'd often have quiche as a side dish with our meals. It was a British influence on our mainly Caribbean Sunday dinners and you'd have it alongside rice, chicken, roast potatoes, coleslaw, plantain and some veggies. As we got older, we started to experiment with some different fillings – the good ol' cheese and ham quiche got a bit boring. This is our new, tasty version. It uses delicious callaloo, sautéed onions and garlic, and is flava'd up with some herbs and spices and topped with soft melted cheese.

There's no pastry, so this super-easy recipe is also gluten-free, but if you want, you can put this same filling in a pastry case and bake it in the usual way.

SERVES 6

1 tbsp olive oil

1 small onion, diced

4 garlic cloves, chopped

1 scotch bonnet pepper, deseeded and diced

½ red bell pepper, deseeded and diced

½ green bell pepper, deseeded and diced

1 x 540g can callaloo, drained well, with excess moisture squeezed out (or use spinach)

2 tsp ground pimento (allspice)

2 tsp dried thyme

1 tsp salt

2 tsp freshly ground black pepper

375g Cheddar cheese, grated

5 eggs

250ml milk

1 tbsp melted butter

Preheat your oven to 160°C Fan/180°C/Gas 4.

Pour the olive oil into a frying pan over a medium-high heat, then add the onion, garlic, scotch bonnet and bell peppers and cook down for 5–7 minutes until soft and a little caramelised.

Add the callaloo and season with the pimento, thyme, salt and black pepper and cook down for 5 minutes until the callaloo is soft. Add half of the grated cheese and mix together well. Tip the mixture into a 23cm quiche dish or ovenproof frying pan.

Beat the eggs in a bowl and add the milk and melted butter, then whisk together to combine. Pour this mixture over the callaloo and sprinkle over the remainder of the grated cheese. Bake in the oven for 35 minutes until set and golden brown.

ROTI

Probably the most popular dish to come out of Trinidad, the roti has a similar shape to a large tortilla wrap, but the method is completely different and uses lots of butter to give it a soft, melt-in-the-mouth texture. The traditional cooking process requires equipment that's not in your everyday kitchen, so we've put our spin on it and created an easy alternative that can be cooked at home in a simple frying pan.

We love going to authentic Trini food spots and eating some good roti with a chana (chickpea) or lentil curry inside, wrapped with the roti bread. Finger-lickin' heaven!

SERVES 4–6 (MAKES 6)

650g plain flour, plus extra for dusting

3 tsp baking powder

¼ tsp salt

400ml water

100ml vegetable oil

1 tbsp melted butter, plus extra for brushing

Mix the flour, baking powder and salt together in a mixing bowl and add the water a likkle at a time until The mixture comes together in a soft dough. Knead into a ball and let sit for 15 minutes.

Dust your work surface with flour, spread the dough out into a medium-sized thick sausage shape, and cut into 6 evenly sized pieces.

Flatten out one piece into a small circle, dust with flour and then, using a rolling pin, roll out into a round as thinly as possible (about 1–2mm) without splitting or tearing the dough. Do this with each piece of dough. Place on a plate, covered with damp kitchen paper.

Mix the oil and the tablespoon of melted butter together. Lightly coat a frying pan with this oil mixture and place over a high heat. Once hot, turn down to a medium–high heat and place a roti in the pan. Cook for 30 seconds or until you see bubbles form on the surface, then turn over the roti and cook on the second side for a further 30 seconds.

Pat the roti down slightly and keep flipping it over, from one side to the other, brushing with the melted butter. Continue until the roti starts to take on some colour.

GREEN SEASONING

This seasoning paste is often used in meat or fish dishes in the Caribbean and its name comes from spicy green scotch bonnet, herbs and spring onions – all ingredients that commonly flavour our food. Traditionally the mixture uses two ingredients that are challenging to find if you're not based in the Caribbean: a Caribbean herb similar to thyme, and shado beni, which is a bit like parsley, so we've replaced these to create a similar, if not exactly the same, taste.

Use this paste as a base seasoning for your meats, or drop into your stews to bring that extra flava.

MAKES 1 JAR

30g fresh coriander leaves (or use basil or oregano, or whatever herb you have)

30g fresh thyme leaves

30g fresh parsley leaves

6 spring onions, sliced

10 garlic cloves, peeled

2 red bell peppers, deseeded and chopped

2 orange bell peppers, deseeded and chopped

2 red onions, chopped

1 tbsp olive oil

A likkle water

A squeeze of lemon or lime juice

2 green scotch bonnet peppers, deseeded

A likkle bit of salt

Blend all ingredients together in a blender to a thick consistency, then strain through a sieve. Place in a sealed jar and keep in the fridge for up to 1 month.

EAT WITH Use to season any meat or fish.

FLAVA TIP You can also freeze this by scooping servings into an ice-cube tray and freezing for up to 2 months. Make sure you defrost it before using.

SCOTCH BONNET PEPPER SAUCE

 A hot, fiery sauce, we sometimes use just yellow scotch bonnets in this recipe as they are said to be the fiercest pepper in Jamaica, but all scotch bonnets produce a distinctive fragrance and delicious taste. Add this sauce to your dishes to bring that extra heat.

MAKES 1 JAR

10 red scotch bonnet peppers

10 orange scotch bonnet peppers

10 yellow scotch bonnet peppers

30g fresh parsley or coriander leaves

A squeeze of lime juice

30ml water, or more if needed

1 tsp salt

Combine all the ingredients in a blender and blitz to a pourable consistency, adding more water if needed. Pour into a jar and seal. Keep in the fridge for 2-4 weeks.

Deseed the scotch bonnets for a less fiery taste.

OUR ENDS

We grew up in South London, along with our 20 cousins – we're all close and some of them come and help us at events. We've many memories of Thornton Heath, CR7, where we came to live with Mum and Dad – meeting friends at the Clock Tower, going to the barbers and the gym, and tasting all the delicious Caribbean food here, including the jerk chicken shop just around the corner. Everything's in walking distance – and the train station, too. Thornton Heath is like a local community, everyone knows each other. If you don't know them personally, you know them by sight, and people respect each other.

Now we run Original Flava, we're lucky to have a good range of shops on our high street to get produce. These shops are a big influence and inspiration, and having a relationship with the shop owners is important to us. We started our business by showing people how to make Caribbean food in easy one-minute videos, so every week we were buying meat and veg from them. Then we began to do a catering deal: five meals for £25 – might be oxtail, curry goat, plantain, chicken curry, fried fish, delivered around London. Good food doesn't have to be expensive if you make it yourself, and having good shops is part of our budgeting process.

Our man Adz is our butcher – we grew up in the same area and now he's with his dad at their shop, Zenith, on Thornton Heath High Street. He's on it, he's on it –

'If a place isn't busy, that means the meat isn't fresh!' As soon as they open at 7am at the weekend, the place is ram-packed with people getting ready to cook their food. We all inspire each other to work hard and he wants to give us the best. Adz chops up lamb neck through the bone for soup – it makes the best stock; he gets us the medium-sized pieces of oxtail we like; and goat or mutton shoulder for curry. Nan taught us that the fleshy part of the goat is the leg – it's more expensive but less bony. You can get a butcher like this to cut pieces through the bone so you get both.

Then there's hard dough bread, bun and cheese, bulla bread and everything else, all made from scratch at Cornfield Bakery. People queue round the corner, especially at Easter for fresh bun and at Christmas time for rum cake. We have a great relationship with the staff and they've known us from

when we were kids. They see how much passion we have for Caribbean food and have let us come and see how they bake at the back of the shop.

After our journey to Jamaica, we can now see lots of similarities between day-to-day life in the Caribbean and our neighbourhood here. The barber we went to there was like the one in Thornton Heath. When you go to the barbers, it's the jokes, music and characters crammed into a small shop. When you are in that torn ten-year-old chair in CR7, it's relaxing but also entertaining – the stories and jokes you hear, you'd think you're in an episode of *EastEnders*. There are friends of the barber who come in every day to say hi and bust jokes and everyone gets a pet name.

He looks like a fish, he's called Fish. He's a bus driver, he's called Driver and big foot is Big Foot. Craig was called Bigz because he was quite podge when he was younger. They called our Dad Pastor because he went to church. When we were in Jamaica, we recognised this attitude and the variations, or nicknames (*'the lingo'*, as they call it there).

Something else: in Jamaica, they have to provide, but it's also about chillin' out and having a good life and whatever makes them happy. In London, everyone's more driven by time and money – all those things that wear us down. Perhaps it's about daylight. There, the sun comes up and you start the day early and always have 12 hours, all year round. But although in London people feel

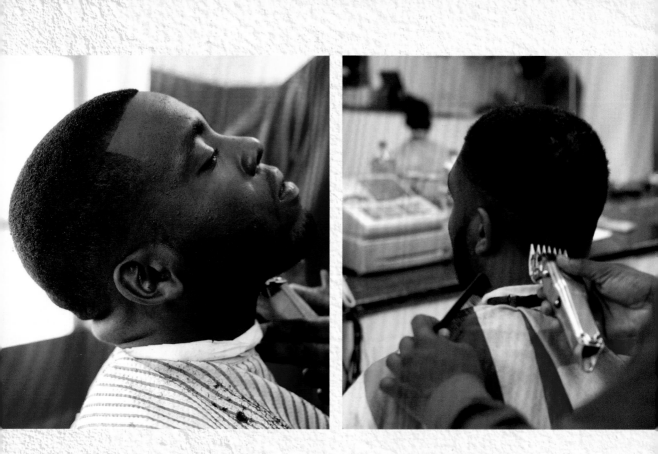

TURN YA HAND AND MEK FASHION

they have less time, where we live, we can still see that way of chillin' in the neighbourhood and sippin' a likkle beverage, similar to those guys on street corners in Jamaica. We're real community-driven people, whether in the Caribbean or here in the UK.

Jamaica is so much more than the place. When you meet a Jamaican, you know they're Jamaican. The personality is so strong it's undeniable. In Britain, the younger generation from all cultures gravitate towards it – they've embraced Jamaican culture in the music, the food, the language, the kids' slang. That confidence comes from the country and the way people think that nothing's a problem. Someone might have very little but you see them and it's *'I'm the best!'* And that's why, though it may be an island thousands of miles away, Jamaica's impact on British and international culture is enormous.

All over Jamaica we found that some of the most amazing dishes were sold on the street, whether in stalls, cook shops, beach shacks or just on carts. We loved eating these dishes and chilling with the locals. Here are our favourites that are good to nyam at meals or as snacks. And CARRRNNNIVALLL! We have so many memories of the Notting Hill Carnival, enjoying the food, people and vibes similar to the carnivals in the Caribbean. Many of these dishes turn up the party atmosphere with delicious on-the-go food. Patties, doubles, grilled seafood – and of course jerk, the all-time Jamaican classic, famous around the world. We're sharing our recipe for home-made jerk sauce and different ways to cook jerk with chicken, pork and veggies, inspired by our trip and seeing and learning about the authentic jerk process. These are perfect recipes to bring DA' FLAVA to your summer BBQs or even to bring some sunshine in di kitchen on a cold winter's day. So get ya friends and family and enjoy di vibes and flavours!

JAMAICAN BEEF PATTIES

The Jamaican beef patty has a flava you won't find in any other cuisine in the world, with a flaky pastry that uses turmeric to give it that Caribbean kick and colour. The aroma makes your mouth-ah wata, as we say! We call patties 'the life of the party' because when people see them they bring that certain excitement that they can't get enough of.

Our grandmother was famous for making patties in Jamaica and we're told our grandad used to eat as many as two or three at a time growing up in Spicy Hill in Trelawny, Jamaica. Yup! We've definitely got his trait as we do the same thing. The secret to the flakiness is to use chilled butter. Member, we tell ya!

MAKES 8–10

FOR THE PASTRY

450g self-raising flour, plus extra for dusting

2 tsp sugar

1½ tsp salt

3 tbsp ground turmeric

30g chilled butter, diced

30g shortening or lard, diced

150–225ml ice-cold water

Milk, for brushing

FOR THE FILLING

1 tbsp vegetable oil

1 medium onion, diced

1 scotch bonnet pepper, deseeded and diced

450g beef mince

½ tsp garlic powder

1 tsp salt

1 tsp freshly ground black pepper

2 beef stock cubes

Sift the flour for the pastry into a bowl then stir in the sugar, salt and turmeric. Add the butter and shortening or lard and rub them into the dry ingredients until you have a crumbly texture. Gradually add enough of the ice-cold water to create a dough. Roll the dough into a ball, wrap in cling film and chill in the fridge for 1 hour.

Meanwhile, for the filling, pour the vegetable oil into a frying pan over a medium–high heat and fry the onion and scotch bonnet for 3 minutes or until soft. Add the beef mince and cook, stirring, until brown. Add the garlic powder, salt and black pepper. Dissolve the beef stock cubes into the boiling water in a jug and add to the pan with the paprika, pimento, breadcrumbs or flour and the soy or other sauce. Stir well and simmer for 20 minutes, then set aside to cool completely.

Preheat the oven to 160°C Fan/180°C/Gas 4.

Take the chilled pastry dough out of the fridge. Dust the work surface with flour to prevent the dough from sticking, and roll out the dough using a rolling pin. Once rolled flat, fold it into a square and roll out again with the rolling pin. Repeat this process 2–3 times; this creates the traditional patty crust.

→

continued overleaf

125ml boiling water

1 tsp paprika

1 tsp ground pimento (allspice)

1 tsp breadcrumbs or flour

2 tbsp dark soy sauce, Worcestershire sauce or browning

Roll out the dough to about a 3mm thickness. Place an upturned bowl, 12–15cm in diameter, on the dough and carefully cut around it using a sharp knife. Repeat to make more rounds; you should be able to get 8–10 in total. Then divide the beef mixture between the pastry rounds, spooning it onto one side of each circle.

Brush a likkle bit of milk around the edge of the dough and carefully fold each patty over so that the edges meet; use your finger to seal them together. Press a fork around the edge of the dough then gently prick the top of the pastry with the fork a few times to make steam holes. Carefully place the patties on a baking tray and bake in the oven for 25 minutes until the pastry is cooked and golden brown. (The patties should be soft but firm on the outside.)

Patties are often served with a range of fillings. Our juicy minced beef is often the most popular, but you could also make them with spicy chicken, saltfish, prawns, vegetables, callaloo – and a really popular one in Jamaica is cheesy beef, which includes melted cheese. To adapt this recipe, you can add grated mature Cheddar or Jamaican canned cheese to your patties (you could use any type of cheese, to be honest), after you spoon your cooked beef mince on the pastry and before you seal the patties.

Add a likkle bit of butter to the filling for extra flava.

DOUBLES

From the islands of Trinidad and Tobago, this deep-fried flatbread is a Caribbean favourite. The warming flavours are an incredible eating experience that makes you go **YAGAH-YO!** With our vegan-friendly chana (chickpea) curry and cucumber chutney, it is heaven on a plate.

SERVES 4 (MAKES 10–12)

Vegetable oil, for cooking
and deep-frying

FOR THE DOUBLES

450g plain flour

1 tsp easy-blend dried yeast

2 tbsp ground turmeric

1 tsp salt

250ml warm water

FOR THE CHANA

2 x 400g cans chickpeas,
drained and rinsed

4 garlic cloves, chopped

1 medium onion, diced

2 spring onions, thinly sliced

1 tsp freshly ground black
pepper

2 tbsp curry powder

½ tsp ground ginger

2 tbsp cornflour

FOR THE CHUTNEY

1 garlic clove, peeled

1 scotch bonnet pepper

Handful of coriander leaves

1 tsp each salt and freshly
ground black pepper

Juice of ½ lemon

1 large cucumber, halved
lengthways, seeds removed
and grated

To make the dough, combine the flour with the yeast, turmeric and salt in a bowl. Mix together. Add enough warm water to form a sticky dough, then knead into a ball, cover with cling film and chill in the fridge for 1 hour.

For the chana, mix the chickpeas with the garlic, onion, spring onions and pepper. Heat 1 tbsp vegetable oil in a deep frying pan, add the curry powder and ginger and cook down over a medium–high heat for a couple of minutes. Add the chickpea mixture to the pan and stir, then cook for 5 minutes. Pour in enough water to cover the chickpeas, and bring to the boil. Mix the cornflour with a likkle cold water to make a paste, then add to the pan, mix and simmer for 15 minutes until thick.

To make the chutney, fling the garlic, scotch bonnet, coriander, salt and pepper into a blender. Squeeze in the lemon and blitz into a puree. It'll smell like fire! Pour this puree over the grated cucumber and mix it up.

To deep-fry the doubles, half-fill a heavy pan with vegetable oil and place over a high heat. Spread a little oil over the dough, break off a walnut-sized piece and roll into a ball, then flatten into a thin round. Repeat with the rest of the dough: you should get 10–12 rounds.

To test if the oil is hot, drop in a piece of bread; if it turns golden in 15 seconds it's hot enough. Working in batches so as not to overcrowd the pan, lower the rounds into the oil and cook for 20 seconds – they will sizzle into puffy flatbreads. Turn them using tongs, and cook for another 10 seconds. Drain on kitchen paper to absorb any oil. Serve with the chana and chutney.

DA' FLAVA JERK BURGER

OMG this beef patty with a blend of Caribbean herbs is **FLAVALICIOUS**. The ultimate juicy jerk burger. There's a real sense of achievement when you create your own burger, plus you can add the toppings of your choice. Dash in some melted cheese, caramelised onions and dripping jerk BBQ sauce and this will definitely have you drooling. The key to a perfect burger is to rest the patty in the fridge to help it to hold together as it cooks. If the weather's good, throw it on the BBQ grill. Sit back, crack open a few drinks and enjoy this super-tasty treat.

MAKES 6

1kg beef mince

2 tsp ground pimento (allspice)

4 tbsp brown sugar

1 tsp ground cinnamon

1 tsp freshly grated nutmeg

1 tsp browning or soy sauce

Squeeze of lime juice

4 garlic cloves, finely chopped

1 medium onion, chopped

2 scotch bonnet peppers, deseeded and diced

2 spring onions, thinly sliced

1 tsp dried thyme

1 tsp freshly ground black pepper

60ml white wine vinegar

1 egg, lightly beaten

Vegetable oil, for cooking

6 square slices of cheese

TO SERVE

6 large lettuce leaves

2 large tomatoes, sliced

1 small onion, sliced into rings

6 burger buns, lightly toasted

Jerk BBQ sauce

Put the beef mince into a mixing bowl and add the pimento, sugar, cinnamon, nutmeg, browning or soy sauce, lime juice, garlic, onion, scotch bonnets, spring onions, thyme, black pepper, vinegar and egg. Mix thoroughly, then divide the mixture into 6 and mould each one into the shape of a burger. Place on a plate or tray, cover and chill in the fridge for 1 hour.

Lightly oil a griddle or frying pan and place over a medium heat. Once hot, dash the burgers on it, in batches of 2 or 3, depending on the size of your pan, and cook on each side until cooked to your preference. Place a cheese square on top of each burger to melt.

Remove the burgers from the pan and keep warm while you sauté the sliced onions in 1 tbsp vegetable oil until well done.

Place a lettuce leaf and some tomato slices on the base of each burger bun, then add a cheese-topped burger, onions and a squeeze of jerk BBQ sauce. If ya bad, top with another burger!

Sweet potato fries or Coleslaw (see page 74).

Use skinless chicken breasts in place of beef mince: marinate for 1 hour in the spice mixture, then cook on the griddle for 5–7 minutes each side until cooked through.

JERK CHICKEN

Jamaican jerk has to be the most succulent chicken you'll ever taste. Many mistake jerk as being all about spice, but this isn't the case. The marinating, smoking and cooking processes make the chicken so tender. On our visit to Jamaica, we tasted the best jerk ever, freshly cooked and foil-wrapped from jerk huts on every corner, across the island. We were spoiled for choice, particularly at Pepperwood's Jerk Centre – the tenderness and taste of their jerk chicken was out of this world! They kindly showed us their authentic process: marinating the meat over two days in dry and wet seasonings, then smoking it over a coal fire on the spiced woods traditionally used to jerk – such as their namesake, pepperwood.

Resources prevent us from doing it like this in the UK, but we have an easy recipe for you to follow that gives a taste just as delicious as the authentic Jamaican recipe. The absolute main event at summer BBQs! We've even got a quick technique if you want to do it in the oven instead.

SERVES 6–8

8 chicken leg and thigh joints

1 tbsp all-purpose seasoning

1 tbsp apple cider vinegar

1 tbsp browning or dark soy sauce

1½ tsp salt

1 tsp freshly ground black pepper

1 tbsp sugar

Juice of 1 lime

1 tsp pimento (allspice) berries

1 tsp ground cinnamon or freshly grated nutmeg

Handful of fresh thyme sprigs

2 spring onions, chopped

1 medium onion, chopped

6 garlic cloves, peeled

2 scotch bonnet peppers

Jerk BBQ sauce, to glaze and serve

Score the chicken pieces with a knife, place in a bowl and massage the all-purpose seasoning into the meat.

Get a blender and dash in all the remaining ingredients except the BBQ sauce. Process until blended, adding a splash of water to help it along. Pour over the chicken and massage it in, letting all them flavas seep into the scores. Cover and marinate overnight in the fridge.

Preheat a charcoal BBQ (one with a lid) and ensure the coal is white and at a medium heat; don't rush it while the coal is black or it will burn up. Place the chicken on the grill skin-side down and cook, turning to ensure it doesn't burn, until cooked through (it needs to reach 75°C when tested with a probe thermometer), dark brown and charred on both sides. Brush jerk BBQ sauce over the chicken to glaze and sit the pieces on the cooler parts of the grill. Close the lid and let them rest for 10 minutes.

Alternatively, preheat the oven to 160°C Fan/180°C/ Gas 4, put the marinated chicken in a roasting tray and fling it in the oven for 25–30 minutes, turning halfway through. Enjoy with extra jerk BBQ sauce and **EAT DI TING!**

JERK BAKED WINGS

Finger-licking spiced wings, the jerk'd up way, this is an on-the-go carnival favourite, especially with a couple of cans of Red Stripe. These go down perfectly, hitting that hunger spot in the best way possible.

If you can, marinate the wings overnight, as the flava is so much better. But don't worry if not – the taste will still leave you craving more.

This method is based on baking the wings in the oven, which is ideal when it's raining and dull outside, which is often in the UK! But if it's Caribbean weather, then throw these tasty marinated wings on the BBQ grill.

SERVES 4-6

1kg chicken wings

Jerk BBQ sauce, to serve

FOR THE JERK MARINADE

1 tbsp apple cider vinegar

1 tbsp browning or dark soy sauce

2 tbsp lime juice

2 tbsp sugar

1 tbsp pimento (allspice) berries

1 tsp freshly ground black pepper

1 tsp ground cinnamon or freshly grated nutmeg

2 tsp fresh thyme leaves

2 spring onions, sliced

2 tbsp chopped fresh ginger

1 medium onion, chopped

6 garlic cloves, peeled

2 scotch bonnet peppers, deseeded

1 tsp salt

50ml water

Dash the jerk marinade ingredients into a blender or food processor and blitz to a thick paste.

Put the chicken wings into a large bowl and add the jerk marinade, turning the wings in the marinade (your hands are best for this) to coat well. If you have time, cover and marinate in the fridge overnight.

When ready to cook, preheat the oven to 200°C Fan/ 220°C/Gas 7. Spread the chicken wings out on a foil-lined baking tray and bake for 45–50 minutes, or until cooked, turning the wings halfway through the cooking time.

Remove and glaze the wings with some jerk BBQ sauce before serving.

 Use chunks of vegetable in place of the chicken wings.

CARIBBEAN BURRITO

Burritos are one of our favourite street foods – outside Caribbean food, of course – so we decided to create our very own flava-filled burrito. Once you nyam one of these, it will get those tastebuds bussin' a dutty whine. **WOW!** This is the Caribbean Ultimate Burrito.

SERVES 4

FOR THE JERK CHICKEN

2 large skinless, boneless chicken breasts

Olive oil, for cooking

6 tbsp jerk BBQ sauce

FOR THE MARINADE

30ml white wine vinegar

1 tbsp browning or dark soy sauce

4 tbsp sugar

5 pimento (allspice) berries

1 tbsp freshly ground black pepper

1 tsp ground cinnamon

Large handful of fresh thyme sprigs

3 spring onions, sliced

1 medium onion, chopped

8 garlic cloves, peeled

2 scotch bonnet peppers (deseeded if you want less heat)

FOR THE FRIED PLANTAIN

2 plantain (look for plantain with dark marks, the more marks the sweeter they are)

Vegetable oil, for shallow-frying

Salt

To make the jerk chicken, put all the marinade ingredients into a food processor or blender and blend to a thick consistency.

Put the chicken breasts into a large bowl. Pour over the marinade and turn to coat, then cover and marinate in the fridge for at least 1 hour, or overnight for best results.

Heat a griddle or frying pan over a medium–high heat. Add a likkle olive oil, then cook the chicken for around 8–10 minutes on each side, or until cooked though. Transfer to a bowl and use a fork to shred the chicken. Add the jerk BBQ sauce and mix together.

For the fried plantain, cut both ends off the plantain then score a line down the middle of the skin and carefully peel open. Slice the plantain on the diagonal. Now put enough oil in a medium frying pan to shallow-fry and set it over a high heat. Fry the plantain slices for 2–3 minutes on each side until golden brown all over. Drain on kitchen paper and sprinkle with salt.

→

continued overleaf

FOR THE RICE AND PEAS

1 x 400g can kidney beans

200ml water

1 tsp salt

1 tsp freshly ground black pepper

1 tsp ground pimento (allspice)

½ medium onion, diced

4 garlic cloves, finely chopped

200ml coconut milk

200g long-grain or basmati rice

1 tsp hot pepper sauce

FOR THE MASHED AVOCADO

2 avocados

A squeeze of lime juice

½ small onion, finely diced

2 medium tomatoes, diced

30g parsley, leaves chopped

1 tsp salt

1 tsp freshly ground black pepper

TO SERVE

4 tortillas

Jerk BBQ sauce

1 lime, cut into wedges

To make the rice and peas, tip the can of kidney beans, with its brine, into a medium saucepan. Add the water, salt, black pepper, pimento, onion, garlic and coconut milk, then bring to the boil and cook for 15 minutes.

Rinse the rice well under cold running water then add to the pan, stir, cover and simmer for about 20 minutes until the rice is cooked. Stir through the hot pepper sauce.

Cut the avocados in half, remove the stones and scoop the flesh into a bowl. Mash using a fork, then add the lime juice, onion, tomatoes, parsley, salt and black pepper and mix together.

To assemble the burritos, warm the tortillas in a dry frying pan. Transfer the warm tortillas to a board and pile equal amounts of the rice and peas and jerk chicken along the middle of each tortilla. Add slices of fried plantain and a generous spoonful of the mashed avocado to each tortilla, then drizzle over some jerk BBQ sauce and finish with a squeeze of lime juice. Roll up each tortilla to make an open-ended burrito by tucking up the bottom edge as you roll.

JERK PORK

A signature Caribbean BBQ and carnival street-food recipe, this is jerk'd-up, tender pork belly cut into juicy cutlets. The key to real jerk is the marinade, a mix of spicy and fragrant ingredients, blended with a dash of sweetness to make the most flavaful mix you'll ever taste. You can use it on meat, fish or veggies and it lasts up to a month in the fridge in a covered jar. Remember, the marinating process is very important to get the maximum flava in your food. If you are really short on time, you can use shop-bought jerk paste – 4 tbsp for this recipe.

The authentic way to cook jerk is over pimento or other scented woods, such as pepperwood, to get a smoked taste – as we witnessed in restaurants on our journey round Jamaica. It's hard to replicate the process at home, but locals gave us some tips on how to get a similar taste. Follow this recipe and you'll get the best jerk pork at home with that succulent texture and the real taste of Jamaica. You can buy pimento wood chips online, and scatter them over the charcoal in the grill, which does give the meat a slightly spiced wood flavour. It's also important to use pimento (allspice) in your jerk paste.

SERVES 4

FOR THE JERK PASTE

70ml apple cider vinegar

1 tsp browning or dark soy sauce

1 tbsp soft brown sugar

50ml lime juice

1 tbsp oil

1 tsp pimento (allspice) berries

1 tsp freshly ground black pepper

1 tsp ground cinnamon or freshly grated nutmeg

Large handful of fresh thyme sprigs

1 medium onion, chopped

2 spring onions, sliced

6 garlic cloves, peeled

2 scotch bonnet peppers

For the jerk paste, put all the ingredients in a blender. (Tek out di seeds from the scotch bonnet if you can't tek di fire!) Add a likkle water and blend to a thick paste, in short bursts, for around 30 seconds.

Put the pork joint in a large bowl, score all over with a knife, so the flava of the seasonings can get inside, and rub all over with jerk seasoning powder and the jerk paste, massaging it into the pork. Cover the bowl with cling film and marinate in the fridge for at least 1 hour, but ideally overnight.

Set up your charcoal BBQ grill and, once the flames have died down and the charcoal has turned grey, place the pork on the grill over a medium heat (not directly over flaming coals), skin-side down. We love a slow-cooked jerk pork, as this is when it's most tender, so it's important the pork isn't over direct flames or it will burn.

→ continued overleaf

1.7kg large pork belly or shoulder joint

2 tbsp jerk seasoning powder

Jerk BBQ sauce, to glaze

Red Stripe or Carib beer, to sprinkle over while grilling (optional)

Cook, turning and glazing the pork with the jerk BBQ sauce every 30 minutes (and sprinkling with beer occasionally, if you like), until brown and crispy on both sides and the inside temperature reads at least 75°C on a meat thermometer. On a slow cook, this can take hours – but be patient, it's worth the wait.

Take the pork off the grill and set aside to rest before using a sharp knife to cut it into small cubes to serve.

Alternatively, you can cook the pork in an oven preheated to 140°C Fan/160°C/Gas 3 for 2¼ hours, then increase the oven temperature to 180°C Fan/ 200°C/Gas 6 and cook for a further 35 minutes.

After marinating the pork, cut it into cutlet-sized pieces, place in an ovenproof frying pan with 1 tablespoon of oil and cook for 10–15 minutes, or until golden all over. It will produce some liquid, but fling in a likkle bit of extra water and cook down for a few minutes. Throw the pan into the oven and cook the pork for around 3 hours until the meat is tender, adding more water if it starts to dry out.

JERK

Jerk is the best known Jamaican food and is eaten all over the world. Many people think of jerk as a spicy sauce, but it's NOT just about the sauce. Jerk is a technique that gives a tenderness to the meat, along with the distinctive seasoning – mainly thyme, spring onion, scotch bonnet and pimento seeds, all classic flavas for us.

At Pepperwood's Jerk Centre, a specialist restaurant in Kingston, we tasted classic Jamaican jerk. Their technique is authentic, marinating the meat for two days, so the flavours seep in, first putting on a dry seasoning of mixed ground spices, and then a wet one with scallions (spring onions) and scotch bonnet. Rather than grilling the meat, they heat pimento wood and lay it on top. With no direct heat, the food is SLOW-cooked – 1½–2 hours for chicken and 3½ hours for pork – and takes on the woodsmoke flavour.

In Jamaica there's the marinating, the smoking and the cooking processes – and then, of course, the eating process! The taste of Pepperwood's jerk is unreal: the best we've ever tasted. That's because we like jerk to be spicy but not TOO hot. What you want, overall, is a good aroma, with a spicy kick, and that's why the smoke works so well. We've found a way to adapt this for home cooks – see page 111 and have a go.

The jerk technique started with Maroons, escaped slaves who fled to the islands and formed their own communities. They used the jerk method to preserve and cook meat from wild pigs over slow-burning fires. These days, jerk is associated with chicken as well as pork – you also get jerk fish and veggies – and there are jerk places everywhere in Jamaica.

Pepperwood's is unusual in the purity of its technique. Most jerk stalls in Jamaica cook the meat over coals in a jerk pan, as we do here in the UK. However the jerk in Jamaica is more tender than we're used to in London takeaways, partly because you get it straight away – as you can do at home – rather than it being cooked in advance and warmed up.

In Jamaica, everyone takes their time with food. Cooking is something they love and take pride in. All over the island, you find individuals on street corners with jerk pans. They start really early and are there all day, often near chillin' spots, or little bars, and also near where cars drive by. So you've got your rum or beer and your jerk in aluminium foil or a polystyrene box. You sit down and eat next to the sizzle and smoke. We know, your belly's probably rumbling right now!

In Jamaica we ate jerk with either rice and peas, hard dough bread, or just by itself. Alongside, you might drink Red Stripe or Magnum – a tonic wine, full of lots of iron to give you nuff stamina.

At Nan's annual birthday BBQ, the family can't get enough of our jerk. There's no taste like a slow-cooked marinated jerk chicken on a jerk pan – the drum BBQ we like to use. Jerk has an incredible history, one that can't be forgotten, and though the cooking equipment may alter, the marinating and variations on the smoking technique create the unique mouth-watering jerk experience that we love and want to share with you.

GRILLED JERK-SEASONED VEGETABLE SKEWERS

Give your veggies some Caribbean FUN with these jerk-seasoned skewers! Made with a range of Caribbean ingredients, these seasoned-up vegetables are chargrilled to create a crisp-edged texture that will make them stand out at your summer BBQs. Ideally done on a BBQ grill, they can also be roasted in the oven and given a chargrilled look by finishing them on a griddle pan on your kitchen hob. Either way, they are pleasing to the eye, especially on a table out in the garden. They're also a good way to get the kids to eat more veggies because the smell and colours will get them excited – if the adults don't get there before then, that is!

SERVES 4 AS A SIDE

2 sweet potatoes

1 yellow bell pepper

1 green bell pepper

1 red bell pepper

2 plantain, peeled

2 corn on the cob

2 red onions

1 small pineapple or 200g canned chunks

2 tbsp olive oil

4 garlic cloves, chopped

2 spring onions, sliced

1 scotch bonnet pepper, deseeded and chopped

Handful of pimento (allspice) berries, crushed

1 tbsp all-purpose seasoning

Handful of thyme sprigs

1 tsp salt

1 tsp freshly ground black pepper

1 tsp soft brown sugar

A squeeze of lime juice, plus extra to serve

Firstly, soften the sweet potatoes slightly by microwaving them for 4–5 minutes. Let them cool.

While the sweet potatoes are cooling, deseed the bell peppers and chop into chunky squares, then cut the plantain and corn into chunky slices. Peel the red onions and cut into wedges. Peel and core the pineapple and cut into chunks. Cut the cooled sweet potatoes into similar-sized chunks.

Put all the remaining ingredients into a large bowl. Mix well, then fling di pineapple, sweet potatoes and other veg into the bowl, mix together and leave to marinate for 20 minutes.

Thread the marinated veg pieces onto skewers (soak wooden ones first to prevent them from catching on the grill). Prepare the BBQ grill or a griddle pan on the stove, and place the skewers on the grill or pan. Cook for 5 minutes, turning, or until nice and charred to your preference. Drizzle lime juice over them and nyam!

EAT WITH Pumpkin Rice (see page 63), fluffy white rice, grilled meat, or just by themselves.

PEPPER PRAWNS

Great tasting, quick-and-easy prawns – made in just 10 minutes – these have a delicious peppery sauce created from Jamaican spices and chilli. A real authentic recipe, it's a favourite in the Caribbean, and one of ours too.

When we were in Jamaica, we often saw people sell pepper prawns on the street in small plastic bags, and locals call them 'swimmers' or 'pepper swims'. They are cooked with the shell on, to create a juicier texture. Some people, like Shaun, take the shells off before eating; others, like Craig, eat them with the shell on. It's totally up to you – either way the flavas are incredible!

SERVES 4 AS A SNACK

1 tbsp vegetable oil

¼ onion, diced

3 garlic cloves, finely chopped

2 scotch bonnet peppers, deseeded and chopped (add more if ya bad!)

450g raw shell-on prawns

Juice of 1 lime

1 tsp freshly ground black pepper

1 tsp all-purpose seasoning

1 tsp paprika

15g parsley leaves, finely chopped

1 tbsp lemon juice

Lemon wedges, to serve

Heat the vegetable oil in a frying pan. When hot, add the onion, garlic and scotch bonnets and cook over a medium heat for 5 minutes.

Wash the prawns with lime juice and some water and trim the legs and antenna, if you like. Add to the pan and cook, stirring, for 2–3 minutes. Add the black pepper, all-purpose seasoning and paprika. Stir and cook for a further 2–3 minutes.

Add the parsley and lemon juice and cook for a further 2 minutes, then serve with lemon wedges.

 This makes a great starter at a dinner party or for a romantic night in.

HONEY HERB SHRIMP NOODLES

This tasty and quick pick-me-up meal will make your mid-week evenings something to look forward to, or provide a Friday-night fakeaway that will stop you spending on overpriced takeaways.

The Chinese in Jamaica have had a big influence on some dishes, and growing up in a Caribbean household, Chinese food was our preferred takeaway on Friday nights. So we've made this dish with an influence from both cultures: the style of the Chinese and the flavours of the Caribbean. With seafood being such a big thing in the Caribbean, this one goes down a treat with our family.

SERVES 4

60g butter

1 tbsp honey

1 tbsp browning or dark soy sauce

1 tsp grated fresh ginger

1 tsp chilli flakes

300g dried egg noodles

½ tbsp olive oil

2 garlic cloves, finely chopped

1 medium onion, finely chopped

1 green bell pepper, deseeded and cut into strips

1 red bell pepper, deseeded and cut into strips

70g raw shelled prawns

Handful of parsley leaves, chopped (optional)

Put the butter and honey in a saucepan and place over a high heat. Mix together, then add the browning or soy and mix to a sauce. Add the grated ginger and chilli flakes, remove from the heat and set aside.

Cook the noodles according to the packet instructions, then drain.

While the noodles are cooking, pour the olive oil into a frying pan, then add the garlic, onion and peppers and sauté for about 5 minutes until softened. Push to one side of the pan and add the prawns to the clear side. Cook for 2–3 minutes on each side until pink and cooked through, then stir in the onion mixture and slowly drizzle the honey sauce over to coat and create a gooey consistency. Serve with the noodles, and chopped parsley if you like.

CURRY CRAB AND DUMPLINGS

Curry crab is sold in Jamaica in massive pots on street corners, with big queues of people waiting to tuck in. It's a favourite in a lot of Caribbean islands, including Guyana and Trinidad – places with an Indian influence. The crab shells create an amazing depth of flavour and even better comes the juicy meat. When you eat the dish, crack open the shells with a lobster cracker, or the back of a knife, then pick out the meat. The dumplings soak up the curry sauce.

SERVES 4

800g crab claws and legs, cleaned and cut into pieces

4 tbsp curry powder

1 tbsp Green Seasoning (see page 86)

1 tsp salt

1 tsp freshly ground black pepper

2 tbsp vegetable oil

1 medium onion, finely chopped

2 spring onions, finely chopped

4 garlic cloves, finely chopped

1 scotch bonnet pepper, deseeded and chopped

1 large tomato, diced

1 tbsp grated fresh ginger

1 tsp ground cumin

1 x 400ml can coconut milk

Lime wedges, to serve

FOR THE DUMPLINGS

400g plain flour

1 tsp salt

200ml water

Place the crab pieces in a large mixing bowl and season with 2 tbsp of the curry powder, the green seasoning, salt and pepper. Mix together and marinate for a few hours in the fridge if you can.

Place a large pan over a medium heat and add the vegetable oil. When the oil is hot, add the onion, spring onions and garlic and sauté until the onions are soft, around 5 minutes. Add the scotch bonnet, tomato, ginger, cumin and 1 tbsp of the curry powder, then cook down for another 2–3 minutes.

Now add the marinated crab pieces to the pan, stirring them around so everyting is coated in the curry base. Pour in the coconut milk and add the remaining 1 tbsp curry powder. Simmer the curry over a medium heat, stirring frequently, for about 10 minutes or until the sauce has thickened.

To make the dumplings, combine the flour and salt in a mixing bowl. Pour in the water and knead the dough into a ball, adding more water or flour as necessary. Break off small pieces of the dough and roll into round dumplings or into long thin shapes – which Jamaicans call 'spinners' – and fling dem into the hot curry. Cook the dumplings in the curry sauce for 10–15 minutes.

You can use a whole crab instead of claws. Ask your fishmonger to remove the back of the crab and thoroughly clean it for you, as this can be tricky.

CURRY PRAWNS

One of the quickest and most flavalicious recipes you'll ever make. Once the prawns have been marinated, this curry is done in about 15 minutes and it tastes fantastic with nothing more than a bowl of rice or noodles. And the plump prawns submerged in the curry is the icing on the cake. Perfect for an easy mid-week dinner to feed the family, or just yourself, with enough to pack away for lunch for the next couple of days.

SERVES 4

400g raw shelled king prawns

2 spring onions, thinly sliced

4 tbsp curry powder

1 tbsp vegetable oil

1 medium onion, finely chopped

4 garlic cloves, finely chopped

1 red bell pepper, deseeded and sliced

1 green bell pepper, deseeded and sliced

1 tsp ground ginger

200ml coconut milk

1 tbsp cornflour

1 tomato ketchup

4 fresh thyme springs

Salt and freshly ground black pepper

Thoroughly wash the prawns. If using frozen prawns, thaw them in cold water.

Pat the prawns dry, score down the back of each prawn with a knife to open it up a bit – this will allow the seasonings to really soak into the prawns and will also make them plump and juicy. Put the prawns in a mixing bowl with the spring onions and season with 2 tbsp of the curry powder, 1 tsp salt and 1 tsp black pepper and mix together. Cover with cling film and leave to marinate for at least 30 minutes, but preferably overnight.

Pour the oil into a frying pan, add the onions, garlic, bell peppers and cook down until they're soft. Then add the remaining 2 tbsp curry powder, the ground ginger and a likkle bit of water. Fling in your prawns, toss around and sauté until the prawns are pink. Pour in the coconut milk, the cornflour mixed with enough water to make a paste, tomato ketchup, thyme sprigs and simmer until the sauce is thickened – this should take a minute or so. Add salt or pepper to taste.

GARLIC BUTTER LOBSTER WITH SWEET CHILLI SAUCE

Jamaicans love seafood, and lobster is one of the most-enjoyed dishes in the Caribbean. This recipe is inspired by Jamaica's butter-herb steamed technique, but with a twist! A buttery-garlic paste infuses the lobster meat, then it's steamed in a sweet-and-spicy sauce. **JEEZ!** Cooking lobster may seem daunting, but – trust us – the process is easy, and the taste is worth it. Getting a cooked lobster isn't hard these days, as you can buy them frozen, so it's just knowing how to prepare it. We've developed this recipe to use the juiciest parts as simply as possible.

SERVES 2

2 cooked lobsters, about 450g each, fresh or frozen (defrosted if frozen)

1 tbsp vegetable oil

1 large onion, diced

1 medium red onion, diced

2 garlic cloves, diced

1 x 400g can chopped tomatoes

4 tbsp white wine vinegar

1 tsp each salt and freshly ground black pepper

3 tsp sugar

½ tsp chilli flakes

1 tbsp all-purpose seasoning

FOR THE GARLIC PASTE

3 tbsp softened butter

4 garlic cloves, minced

2 spring onions, thinly sliced

Bunch of parsley, finely chopped

1 tsp dried thyme

½ scotch bonnet pepper, deseeded and diced

1 tsp each salt and freshly ground black pepper

For the garlic paste, throw the ingredients into a bowl and mash down using a fork, creating a thick paste.

To split each lobster, uncurl the tail and hold the body firmly on a board. Using a sharp knife, pierce the lobster shell at the centre point where the head joins the body, then bring the knife down through the head along the centre seam. Now cut the other way, from the base of the head along the length of the body, again along the centre seam down to the tail. Open it up and remove the stomach sac with a spoon. Crack open the claws using the back of a heavy knife. Stuff the garlic paste into the shells and chill for 1 hour.

Heat the oil in a frying pan, add both types of onion and the garlic and cook over a medium heat for 3–5 minutes until soft. Dash in the tomatoes, vinegar, salt, pepper, sugar, chilli flakes and all-purpose seasoning. Pour in a likkle water to give it a more saucy look.

Place the lobster halves shell-side down in the sauce, so they are nestling in the sauce but sitting just proud of it, and simmer for 10 minutes until they have warmed through and the garlic paste has melted into the lobster meat. Alternatively, place the sauce and lobster in a roasting tray and warm through on a BBQ.

EAT WITH Yam Mash (see page 75), roasted baby potatoes, fries or white rice and vegetables.

ROAST SEAFOOD MIX

This is inspired by an outrageously tasty seafood dish in Jamaica: roast conch. Conch is taken out of its shell and first grilled or boiled, then either stewed down or baked in foil with a mixture of vegetables. It's a hidden gem that's well loved by people who know about it.

Craig had some in Jamaica and raves about it all the time, so we decided to make a variation with scallops as a more easily accessible seafood alternative. They are similar in texture and taste, and both work really well with the seasonings in this recipe.

SERVES 2

400g scallops (no corals)

1 tbsp salt

1 tsp freshly ground black pepper

1 tsp fresh thyme leaves

3 garlic cloves, finely chopped

3 spring onions, sliced

1 medium onion, diced

1 scotch bonnet pepper, deseeded and diced

Handful of okra, chopped

½ tsp browning or dark soy sauce

250g carrots, finely grated

60ml olive oil

½ cho cho (chayote), peeled, cored, and finely diced (optional)

Cut the scallops into quarters, then place in a bowl with all the remaining ingredients and mix together. Cover with cling film and marinate in the fridge for 4 hours, or preferably overnight.

Tear off two sheets of foil, each large enough to wrap half of the scallop mixture. Lay out the foil and divide the scallop mixture between the sheets, then wrap the foil up tightly to make airtight parcels.

Set up your BBQ grill, or preheat your oven to 160°C Fan/180°C/Gas 4. Place the foil parcels on the grill on a baking tray or in the oven and cook for around 10–15 minutes.

CALYPSO SALAD

A crunchy and flavasome salad, this is perfect for summer BBQs. Sometimes salads can be given a miss at parties but here we've used inspiration from Caribbean coleslaw and traditional salad recipes to make a dish that's splashed with tropical colours and will get your guests excited to dive in.

SERVES 4 AS A SIDE

1 large white cabbage, sliced

¼ red cabbage, sliced

2 carrots, sliced

1 medium onion, thinly sliced

½ red bell pepper, deseeded and sliced

½ green bell pepper, deseeded and sliced

½ scotch bonnet pepper, deseeded and diced

1 x 165g can sweetcorn, drained

Handful of fresh parsley leaves

1 tbsp olive oil

Juice of 2 limes

1 tbsp salad cream

A likkle salt

A likkle freshly ground black pepper

1 tsp dried thyme

1 tbsp honey (optional)

Put all the prepared vegetables in a bowl with the sweetcorn and parsley leaves, then mix together with the olive oil and lime juice.

Add the salad cream, thyme, honey (if using), and salt and black pepper and stir gently to coat all the veg.

FESTIVAL

A feel-good snack, festival is similar in taste and texture to a dumpling – but it's made with cornmeal, is much sweeter and is rolled into a thick, sausage shape. We like to call this the uncle of fried dumplings, as it's bigger and more seasoned with experience, you could say!

In the Caribbean, festival is often fried in a big pot alongside fried fish and bammy, as they are all often eaten together. We love to eat it with a curry, as it tastes delicious after it's dunked in a flava-filled sauce. It's also a great party snack to tuck into before the main course. Don't be surprised if you end up nyammin' several of these at one time!

SERVES 4 (MAKES 8)

250g fine cornmeal

450g plain flour

3 tsp baking powder

A likkle salt

3 tsp sugar

1 tsp vanilla extract

300–350ml water

Vegetable oil, for shallow-frying

Put the cornmeal and flour into a bowl and stir together. Add the baking powder, salt, sugar and vanilla, then mix together.

Gradually add enough water to bring the mixture together into a dough. Form into a large ball, wrap in cling film and leave to rest in the fridge for 30 minutes.

Cut the rested dough into 8 pieces and carefully roll each one into a long, thick sausage shape.

Pour a 3cm depth of oil into a frying pan and place over a high heat. The oil should be hot – but not piping hot – before you add the festival. (If the oil is giving off smoke, it's too hot.)

Place a few festival in the pan and turn down the heat to medium. Cook until they are golden brown on both sides. Drain the cooked festival on kitchen paper to soak up the excess oil while you cook the rest.

Any curry dish, to dip into the flavalicious curry sauce and nyam. **JEEZ!**

FISH SHACKS, FOOD STALLS & COOK SHOPS

Wherever you go in Jamaica, you find something good to eat – likkle jerk huts, food stalls and carts, cook shops, zinc-roof beach shacks selling seafood – and all of them vibrant with colourful painted walls, such as the red, gold and green of Rasta, the Jamaican flag colours, and natural sea-blue and bright yellow.

In Jamaica, it's so hot inside that people often cook outside. There's a lot of food preparation done on the street, and the community's so good that people passing by day-to-day talk with the shopkeepers and stall holders in their passionate patois. A lot of cooks make their own grills, perhaps from wheel rims or whatever's around – like the jerk pans made from oil drums; most is make-do and improvised and it works.

The famous seafood of Jamaica is cooked fresh at stalls on the white sands and roadsides along the coast. On the first day, we saw a bunch of just-caught fish hanging in a tree waiting for the coals to heat up, so we pulled up for some lunch. The fisherman gave us our first roast conch – JEEZ! This was a new taste for us, and a Jamaican classic. He got the flesh out of the shell, grilled it over coals, and then steamed it in a foil parcel with a mix of veg such as peppers, spring onions, okra and herbs. (Check our recipe, using scallops, on page 130.) You can also have it brown stewed-down, curried or in a soup.

One of the highlights of our journey was Hellshire Beach, on the south coast near Kingston. It was off-season, so like a deserted town full of food shacks next to natural, beautiful beaches. Some shacks are no longer occupied but still stand there, with Jamaican legends and symbols painted on the outside – Bob Marley, Haile Selassie and Paul Bogle, the Baptist minister and Jamaican national hero who led a protest against poverty and injustice.

These places do crab, lobster, snapper and other whole fish – everyone does everyting. The fishermen go out at night and come back after dawn, so you get the seafood caught and cooked fresh. Our lunch was at a place run by a man called Genna Genna, where we ate fried parrot fish. His pan of oil was heated over a wood fire – our nan grew up cooking on a wood fire – and first he heated up a scotch bonnet pepper to flavour the oil. The fish tasted so sweet; sweeter than parrot fish we've had in London, and so fresh and tasty. He served it with festival fried in the same oil. We were also shown how to make curry crab and got a recipe.

We stopped off at a great run of food places between Discovery Bay and Runaway

Bay, in St Ann. The first attraction was the famous pudding man, Edgar, and his four types of pudding, including sweet potato and pumpkin, all made on a row of coal stoves outside the shop. He puts his pudding in a pot with a lid and heats it with coals above and below. The saying goes that it's *'Hell a-top, hell a-bottom and Hallelujah in the middle!'* A bit further down the road is a great cook with her cook shop, and we knew her food would be good: they say the bigger the arms, the better the cook. We tried her banana fritters and then she opened up her jerk pan to show us a row of pots keeping warm, all full of good foods – brown stew pork and chicken, rice and peas, jerk chicken and fried chicken, ackee and saltfish, and hard food. YA MON!

Every food seller have their little ting. Yammie was the guy with a stall where he grows his own vegetables, including callaloo and okra. Here we ate breadfruit charred in a jerk pan and with plenty of butter – we'd never had it with butter before, and it tasted delicious served with fish. People also cook breadfruit over coals – we got that recipe too. Because it's really hot, you handle it with wet newspaper or a towel, or at home use oven gloves over the gas flame. Yammie got us preparing some ackee. This iconic Jamaican ingredient is only sold in cans in the UK, and it was here that we saw and ate them fresh for the very first time.

Markets often have good street food and we found plenty around Coronation Market in Kingston, where there were bubbling pots of chicken soup and white rice seasoned with curry powder and spring onions. All over the island we often saw soup cooked up by locals on street corners. You can see the

smiles on the customers' faces, who line up while the soup maker stirs around the big pot of soup, perhaps filled with tender meat, soft vegetables and dumplings coated in the rich stock that is made by the stewed-down red kidney beans.

Then there was the Porridge Man. From his cart we ate cornmeal and green banana porridge that was so amazing we couldn't put it down. He had lines from the Bible painted on the cart because people want blessings to come to their business – it reminded us of the kitchen prayers found on walls in Jamaican homes all over the world.

The range of food stalls you get in Jamaica is found in London at the Notting Hill Carnival in August. Here you get the best of Caribbean street food: patties, curry goat, roti, jerk chicken and pork with hard dough bread. The cooks in London have more equipment such as big electric and gas stoves. In Jamaica, they might not have these but they make great food because of their skill and their love for what they're making – community is such an important source of joy and satisfaction, so everyone tends to be a cook. Their good food brings a sense of happiness, friendliness and togetherness; we also know, from our own business, about the hard graft of making food and making a living. The people of Jamaica... Land we love! Food we love!

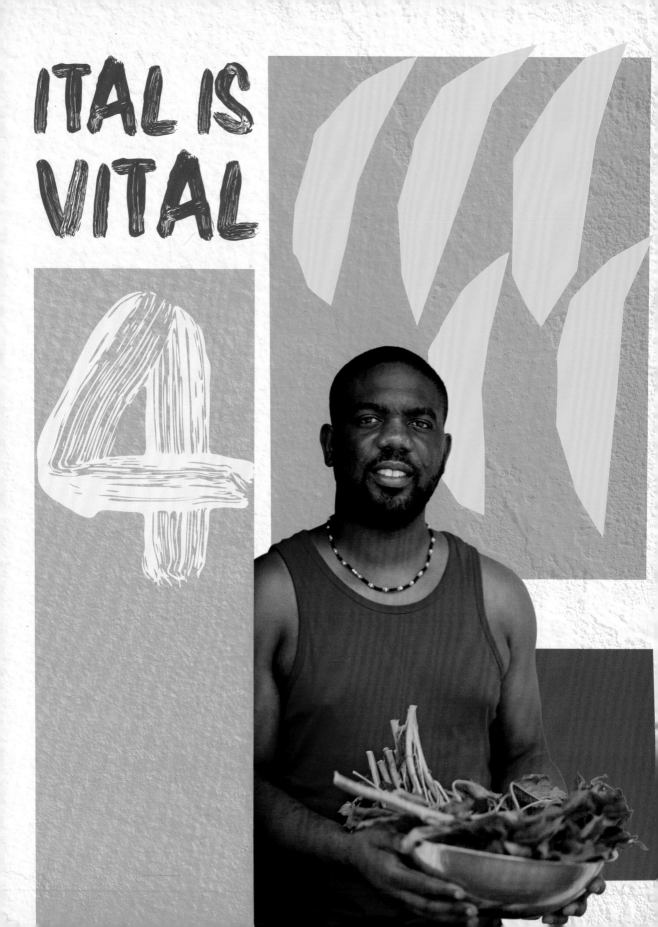

ITAL IS
VITAL

4

Ital is a Rasta way of eating that is healthy, natural and vegan. The thing we love about Caribbean plant-based dishes is the bountiful flavas from veggies mixed in with the herb and spice seasonings we use to make our food taste so good. On our travels to Jamaica, we witnessed the abundance of fresh vegetables and fruit such as ackee, breadfruit and more growing in our nan's back garden, or even just on the side roads, and were inspired by how the locals make this produce into great dishes. When you eat less meat, you pay more attention to other ingredients, and a little care and a lot of flava makes these dishes extra special, all using ingredients that are easily accessible in local supermarkets. Our Ital stews will fill you up in the best way, and our Vegan Dinner Bowl is a feast for your eyes, belly and health. Then there are some non-meat spins on dishes such as Lentil Bolognese, Plantain Beanburgers and Jamaican Stew Peas. Vegan isn't boring, mon – it is FRESH and ITAL.

COOK-DOWN ACKEE AND CALLALOO

A delicious and nourishing vegan dish, this is made of two ingredients that are usually cooked separately and eaten for breakfast in the Caribbean. We love to combine them for a dish that we eat at any time of day, as they always give a satisfying feeling – we particularly love the amazing natural taste of ackee.

It's really easy to make – around 10 minutes – as ackee and callaloo are bought here in cans, though you can get fresh callaloo from markets close to Caribbean communities. When we were in Jamaica, we'd see the ackees growing on the trees, and the callaloo growing in the fields – a beautiful sight.

If you're after trying a true Caribbean vegan dish, we recommend eating this with some dumplings. Give it a go, get that **VEGAN FLAVA!**

SERVES 4–6

2 tbsp vegetable oil

1 scotch bonnet pepper, deseeded and diced

1 large onion, diced

2 spring onions, thinly sliced

4 garlic cloves, finely chopped

1 x 540g can callaloo, or 500g fresh

1 medium tomato, chopped

1 red bell pepper, deseeded and finely diced

1 yellow bell pepper, deseeded and finely diced

1 green bell pepper, deseeded and finely diced

5 fresh thyme sprigs, leaves only

1 tsp ground pimento (allspice)

1 tsp salt

2 tsp freshly ground black pepper

2 x 540g cans ackee, drained

Heat the oil in a frying pan over a medium heat, then add the scotch bonnet, onion, spring onions and garlic and cook for 3 minutes until soft.

Add the callaloo to the pan, then the tomato, bell peppers, thyme leaves, pimento, salt and half of the black pepper. Cook down for 2–3 minutes, then add the drained ackee and remaining black pepper and stir gently; be very careful when stirring – nobody likes mushy ackee. Simmer for 5 minutes before serving.

Fried Plantain (see page 37), Fried Dumplings (see page 40), Rice and Peas (see page 59), hard food (see page 23), or as part of a Vegan Dinner Bowl (see page 161).

ITAL RUNDOWN

Rundown is a Jamaican name for a curried-down dish using coconut milk. This one has to be one of our favourites, packed with our fave sliced Caribbean veggies that make the dish full of flavour and comfort. Whoever said vegan is boring? Look pon dis!

To get the best out of the flavours of the veggies, the timing is key as some take longer to cook than others. Rundown has to be more about the veg than the sauce, which should be plentiful with ingredients.

SERVES 4–6

1 tbsp vegetable oil

1 medium onion, diced

4 garlic cloves, finely chopped

1 scotch bonnet pepper, deseeded and finely diced

1 tsp freshly ground black pepper

Handful of fresh thyme sprigs

Thumb-sized piece of fresh ginger, peeled and finely diced

1 tsp ground pimento (allspice)

200g sweet potato, peeled and cut into small chunks

200g pumpkin or butternut squash, peeled, deseeded and cut into small chunks

1 large corn on the cob, cut into 4–6 segments

½ cho cho (chayote), cored and cut into thin wedges

200ml vegetable stock

1 each of red, yellow and orange bell peppers, deseeded and sliced

100g greens (such as kale or spinach)

200ml coconut milk

Firstly add the vegetable oil to a pan over a high heat and sauté the onion, garlic and scotch bonnet for around 5 minutes until soft.

Add the black pepper, thyme, ginger and pimento and stir them in, then add the sweet potato, pumpkin or squash, corn, cho cho and stock. Bring to the boil and cook for around 15 minutes until the veg are soft.

Add the peppers and greens and mix together, then add the coconut milk, give it a stir and simmer for 5 minutes before serving.

EAT WITH Hard food (see page 23) or white rice.

BUTTER BEAN, SWEET POTATO AND OKRA STEW

A warm, flavoursome stew, this is packed with hearty and delicious ingredients, and is quick and easy to cook – a midweek pick-me-up and a great way to flavour up your veggies. We like to eat this not only on the day it's cooked but also the next day too, because the flavas marinate incredibly well into the vegetables. The seasonings, and the chopped tomatoes with a touch of coconut, make it really good – tasty, thick and perfect with some fluffy rice or pasta.

SERVES 4

1 tbsp vegetable oil

1 red onion, chopped

½ scotch bonnet pepper, deseeded and diced (or seeds left in for a fiery kick)

3 garlic cloves, chopped

1 tbsp curry powder

1 tsp ground turmeric

1 tsp ground ginger

200ml water

500g sweet potatoes, peeled and cut into 2.5cm dice (450g prepared weight)

1 x 400ml can coconut milk

1 x 400g can chopped tomatoes

2 bay leaves

1 x 400g can butter beans, drained and rinsed

Handful of okra, chopped

Handful of chopped coriander or parsley, to serve

Pour the vegetable oil into a pan and dash in the red onion, scotch bonnet and garlic. Cook over a medium heat for around 5–7 minutes until soft, then fling in the curry powder, turmeric, ginger and a likkle bit of the water and cook down for a couple of minutes.

Throw in the sweet potatoes and toss for a couple of minutes until fully coated in the curry paste and lightly caramelised. Tip in the coconut milk, tomatoes, bay leaves and remaining water and cook up di ting for 10 minutes. Once the potatoes are semi-soft, dash in the butter beans and chopped okra and cook for a further 5 minutes.

When it's ready, fling some chopped coriander or parsley pon it. **TING DUN!**

White rice, pasta or bread.

You can add in more veggies if you wish, or red beans or lentils.

Leave out the coconut milk and add some coconut shavings instead.

COCONUT ITAL STEW

This was the first-ever vegan recipe we developed and put online – we loved it, and so did our awesome online family. It's got a load of bulky vegetables stewed down to make the thickest of stews. The superpower in this one is the plantain and, if you can find a ripe one, defo go for that as the sweetness will introduce a flavaful addition to the other nutritious veggies. This goes well with rice or a slice of bread.

SERVES 4–6

1 tbsp vegetable oil

1 large onion, chopped

½ small red onion, chopped

2 tsp finely chopped garlic

2 tsp finely chopped ginger

2 tsp curry powder

2 tsp paprika

300g pumpkin or butternut squash, peeled, deseeded and cut into 2–3cm chunks (250g prepared weight)

200g sweet potatoes, peeled and chopped

1 x 400ml can coconut milk

500ml water

2 tsp freshly ground black pepper

1 cho cho (chayote), cored and cut into chunky wedges

100g yellow yam, peeled and cut into chunks

1 scotch bonnet pepper

Handful of fresh thyme sprigs

2 vegetable stock cubes or 1 tbsp vegan stock granules

2 plantain, peeled and sliced

8–10 okra, sliced into rings

Handful of parsley, chopped

Salt

Heat the oil in a large pot, then add both types of onion and the garlic and sauté for 2 minutes. Add the ginger and sauté for 1 minute, then add the curry powder and paprika. Cook for 2 minutes over a medium heat before adding the pumpkin or squash, sweet potatoes and coconut milk.

Add the water along with the black pepper and salt to taste, and stir to mix. Simmer for 20 minutes until the pumpkin and sweet potatoes are soft, then add the cho cho, yam, scotch bonnet and thyme and mix together. Add the stock cubes or granules and cook for 15 minutes, then add the plantain and okra and simmer for a further 5 minutes.

Remove the whole scotch bonnet, season to taste and garnish with the parsley to serve.

PLANTAIN AND CHICKPEA CURRY

A thick and flavaful curry, this is one of our most-loved vegan dishes when we do food events – people always come back for more. A tasty base is important to make the perfect curry, so we first create a paste by lightly caramelising finely diced onion with garlic, spices and a likkle bit of water. This then combines with a great balance of other ingredients: the chickpeas absorb flavours well and go with the sweetness of the plantain and nutritious callaloo. It's a great-tasting one-pot meal that can also be eaten with rice to make it go further.

SERVES 4

1 tbsp vegetable oil

1 medium onion, finely diced

4 garlic cloves, finely chopped

1 tbsp grated fresh ginger

1 tsp ground cumin

2 tbsp dried mixed herbs

1 tbsp chilli powder

1 tsp all-purpose seasoning

6 tbsp curry powder

125ml water

200ml coconut milk

2 x 400g cans chickpeas, drained and rinsed

4 ripe plantain, peeled and sliced

1 scotch bonnet pepper

3 spring onions, sliced

1 tsp salt

1 tbsp freshly ground black pepper

150g fresh callaloo or spinach

Heat the oil in a pot over a medium heat, then add the onion, garlic and ginger and sauté for 5–7 minutes until the onion is soft. Add the cumin, mixed herbs, chilli powder, all-purpose seasoning, 4 tbsp of the curry powder and a tiny bit of the water; stir together. Add just a tiny bit of the coconut milk and mix together to form a paste.

Add your chickpeas, plantain and scotch bonnet and mix into the curry paste, then add the rest of the water and coconut milk and stir.

Add the spring onions and remaining curry powder, along with the salt and black pepper, then stir, cover with a lid and simmer for 15 minutes.

After that give it a mix and add your callaloo or spinach, then stir gently. Simmer for a further 5 minutes before removing the scotch bonnet and serving.

EAT WITH

Rice and Peas (see page 59), Roti (see page 84) or white rice.

YAM AND PUMPKIN CURRY

A softly spiced curry that offers a warm and gentle taste, this is great for everyone in the family, and a really easy dish to make. Yam and pumpkin are starchy, wholesome veggies, so when curried down they produce a good thick sauce and a filling vegan dish.

SERVES 4

2 tbsp coconut oil or olive oil

1 medium onion, diced

4 garlic cloves, chopped

3 spring onions, sliced

2 tbsp curry powder

1 tsp ground turmeric

200ml coconut milk

300g yellow yam, peeled, cut into bite-sized chunks and rubbed with lime to prevent discoloration (250g prepared weight)

300g pumpkin or butternut squash, peeled, deseeded and cut into bite-sized chunks (250g prepared weight)

1 tsp paprika

2 tsp all-purpose seasoning

1 tsp salt

2 tsp freshly ground black pepper

3 fresh thyme sprigs

1 scotch bonnet pepper

Handful of coriander or parsley leaves, to serve

Heat the oil in a pot over a high heat. Add the onion, garlic and spring onions and sauté for 2 minutes. Add the curry powder and turmeric and cook for 3 minutes, then add just a little of the coconut milk and stir together to make a paste.

Add the yam and pumpkin or squash and stir to coat in the paste before adding the paprika, all-purpose seasoning, salt and black pepper. Mix together, then pour in enough water to just cover the veg. Boil for 20 minutes until the yam and pumpkin are soft.

Add the rest of the coconut milk, the thyme and scotch bonnet and simmer for 5 minutes. Remove the scotch bonnet, sprinkle coriander or parsley leaves over the top and serve.

Hard food (see page 23), Rice and Peas (see page 59), white rice or steamed vegetables.

Alternatively, combine with a variation of other vegan recipes, such as Cook-Down Ackee and Callaloo (see page 142) and Roasted and Fried Breadfruit (see page 206) to make a flavaful platter.

ROASTED VEGETABLE CURRY

Nanny always tells us *'No food fi waste!'* This basically means, *'Don't waste your food!'* We've grown up with that mentality, so in this delicious roasted vegetable curry recipe we use all the veggies, even the skins, so there's no need to peel. Keep the skin on nuh mon!

SERVES 3–4

150g butternut squash, skin on

150g sweet potatoes, skin on

150g waxy potatoes, such as Charlotte, skin on

Olive oil, for cooking

1 medium onion, diced

1 medium red onion, diced

4 garlic cloves, chopped

3 spring onions, sliced

Thumb-sized piece of fresh ginger, peeled and finely chopped

2 large tomatoes, chopped

3 tbsp curry powder

1 tsp paprika

100ml coconut milk

100ml vegetable stock

Large handful of fresh thyme sprigs

Handful of fresh callaloo or spinach

1 scotch bonnet pepper

Salt and freshly ground black pepper

Preheat the oven to 160°C Fan/180°C/Gas 4.

First wash your squash, sweet potatoes and potatoes and cut up into 3.5cm chunks (deseeding the squash). Put on a baking tray then drizzle over about 1 tbsp olive oil, season with salt and black pepper and mix together. Roast in the oven for 30 minutes until tender.

Heat another 1 tbsp olive oil in a large frying pan over a high heat, then add both onions, the garlic, spring onions, ginger and tomatoes. Lower the heat and cook down for 5–7 minutes until soft, then add 1 tsp salt, 1 tbsp black pepper, the curry powder and paprika. Mix together and cook for 1 minute, then stir through the coconut milk to make a thick paste.

Now take the roasted vegetables out of the oven and add to the frying pan. Mix together, then add the stock, thyme, callaloo or spinach and scotch bonnet. Cook down for 3–5 minutes until bubbling hot. Remove the scotch bonnet before serving.

CURRY TOFU

Nowadays tofu is often found in restaurants around the UK, but outside the Rastafarian culture, vegan dishes aren't so prevalent in Jamaica. Across the island, we did see curry tofu being offered as one of the main non-meat options at some food stalls. With curries so popular in Jamaica, this way of preparing tofu is an ideal way to introduce more non-meat dishes to islanders. Without doubt, the flavours from this dish will make your tastebuds **STAN'UP!** And tofu is quick to cook, another positive on top of all the tasty flavours in here.

If your tofu comes in a pack with liquid and is quite moist, you'll have to dry it first (see the method below). Then you're ready to curry up di ting!

SERVES 4

280g firm tofu

1 tbsp olive oil

1 medium onion, diced

4 garlic cloves, chopped

1 tbsp curry powder

1 tsp freshly ground black pepper

1 tsp grated fresh ginger

1 scotch bonnet pepper, deseeded and diced

Large handful of fresh thyme sprigs

3 spring onions, sliced

2 large tomatoes, diced

1 x 400ml can coconut milk

First you need to open the packet of tofu and drain off the liquid. To dry the tofu further, pat it with kitchen paper then put it onto a plate, cover with another plate and leave it in the fridge to drain for at least 1 hour.

When you're ready to cook, cut the drained tofu into 2–3cm cubes.

In a large frying pan, heat the olive oil, add the onion and garlic and cook down for 5–7 minutes over a medium heat until soft.

Dash in di curry powder, along with the black pepper and ginger. Cook until browned, then add the scotch bonnet, thyme, spring onions and tomatoes and stir di ting. Add the coconut milk and stir again.

Add the cubed tofu to the pan and simmer for 10 minutes before serving.

 White rice.

STEW PEAS

A mouth-watering, thick stew, this is filled with tasty vegetables and soft dumplings called spinners, which are small, thin dumplings that balloon up when boiled. Another feature is that the kidney beans (which Jamaicans refer to as 'peas') are soaked and boiled to give the dish that signature Jamaican stew peas red-brownish colour, but if you're short of time you can use canned. Traditionally, the recipe for stew peas includes meat, but we've removed this to make a vegan dish – there's so much flavour already that meat doesn't have to be the star attraction.

SERVES 4

500g dried kidney beans, or 2 x 400g cans

250ml water (if using dried beans)

4 garlic cloves, peeled

Handful of fresh thyme sprigs

5 pimento (allspice) berries

2 spring onions, halved

1 tsp salt

1 tbsp freshly ground black pepper

1 x 400ml can coconut milk

2 large potatoes, peeled and cut into 2–3cm cubes

400g pumpkin or butternut squash, peeled, deseeded and cut into 2–3cm cubes

3 large carrots, sliced

4 medium tomatoes, chopped

1 scotch bonnet pepper

FOR THE SPINNERS

250g plain flour

½ tsp salt

100ml water

If using dried kidney beans, you first need to soak them overnight in plenty of cold water.

Next day, drain and rinse the soaked beans, then add to a large pot with the 250ml water. Bring to the boil, then add the garlic, thyme, pimento seeds, spring onions, salt, black pepper and coconut milk. Cover with a lid and boil for about 30 minutes over a high heat. If using canned kidney beans, just tip the contents of the cans into the pan, add the other ingredients (no need for the water) and bring to the boil.

Take off the lid (the dried beans should be halfway cooked at this stage), add a likkle water if needed, then add your potatoes, pumpkin or squash, carrots, tomatoes and scotch bonnet, cover again and simmer for a further 30 minutes.

Now start making the spinners. Put the flour and salt in a bowl and gradually add the water, kneading it into a dough. Break off a walnut-sized piece of dough and use both hands to twist into a mini sausage shape. Make as many as you can and set aside.

Uncover the pot (at this stage the dried beans should be soft; taste one to check). Carefully take out the scotch bonnet because we don't want it to burst! Add some water if needed, then dash in the dumpling spinners and put the lid back on the pot. Cook for a further 15 minutes until the spinners are cooked.

VEGAN DINNER BOWL

A flavalicous array of Caribbean goodness, all in one bowl, this mixture of crunchy, soft and creamy food makes your belly say **YA MON!** It's one of our absolute favourite things to eat. This bowl of pure Caribbean flava was inspired by the vegan platters we ate at Rastaman Ade's vegan restaurant, just off Negril Beach in Jamaica – they're the largest plates you'll ever see. We were welcomed into their kitchen to meet the cooks, who were super-cool and gave us their secret tips. So nuff respect to the guys at Rastaman Ade's. If you're in Negril, check them out.

SERVES 4

½ quantity each Rice and Peas (see page 59), Curry Tofu (see page 156), Stew Peas (see page 158) and Plantain Fritters (see page 283)

1 avocado, stoned and sliced

salt and freshly ground black pepper

FOR THE SLAW

1 large white cabbage, sliced

2 carrots, sliced

½ red bell pepper, deseeded and sliced

½ scotch bonnet pepper, deseeded and diced

1 tbsp olive oil

Juice of 2 limes

FOR THE CALLALOO

1 tbsp vegetable oil

1 medium onion, diced

4 garlic cloves, finely chopped

½ each red and green bell peppers, deseeded and diced

1 scotch bonnet pepper, deseeded and diced

1 x 540g can callaloo

1 tsp dried thyme

1 large tomato, chopped

For the slaw, put all the prepared vegetables in a bowl, then mix together with the olive oil and lime juice. Add salt and black pepper and stir gently to coat the veg.

For the callaloo, pour the vegetable oil into a frying pan over a high heat, then add the onion, garlic, bell peppers and scotch bonnet and sauté for 2–3 minutes. Lower the heat, add the callaloo and cook for a further 5 minutes, then fling in the tomato and season with salt and black pepper to taste. Mix together and simmer for another 5 minutes.

For the plantain fritters, follow the recipe given for Banana Fritters on page 283, using overripe plantain instead of banana.

Using a sharp knife, slice through the avocado lengthways until you feel the knife hit the stone. Open up the avocado and remove the stone. If dicing, score the flesh of the avocado without piercing the skin. If slicing, scoop out the flesh and then cut into slices.

When ready to serve, reheat the Rice and Peas, Curry Tofu and Stew Peas if necessary. Make sure they are steaming hot all the way through, and do not reheat them more than once. To assemble your vegan dinner bowl, spoon out a portion of each of the separate dishes, placing them close to each other but not mixing them together. Top with the sliced avocado.

PLANTAIN BEANBURGER

We've added a Caribbean twist to this delicious burger, made from smashed black beans and plantain. Make sure you use ripe plantain – with black skin – and mash up di ting! Seasoned up, it's then formed into a juicy plant-based burger to put on the grill. Bring da' flava to your vegan life!

SERVES 4

2 tbsp coconut oil or olive oil

1 medium onion, chopped

2 ripe plantain (choose ones with black spots), peeled

1 x 400g can black beans, drained

1 tsp salt

1 tsp freshly ground black pepper

1 scotch bonnet pepper, deseeded and finely diced

1 tsp dried thyme

2 tbsp finely chopped parsley

1 tsp paprika

2 garlic cloves, finely chopped or grated

250g porridge oats or plain flour

1 tbsp lime juice

TO ASSEMBLE

4 x burger buns (vegan-friendly, if you like), to serve

Shredded iceberg lettuce

Sliced tomato

Sliced avocado

Sweet chilli sauce

Heat 1 tbsp of the oil in a small pan over a medium heat, add the onion and cook for 10 minutes until soft and caramelised, then set aside.

If you have a food processor, great! Put in all the burger ingredients, including the caramelised onion, and whizz up to combine.

If not, no problem mon. Just grab a mixing bowl and mash down the plantain; if you have slightly firmer plantain, you can boil them down to soften and make the mashing process easier. Add the black beans to the bowl and mash with the plantain, then add some flava with the salt, black pepper, scotch bonnet, thyme, parsley, paprika, garlic and your softened onions. Add the oats or flour, then sprinkle in the lime juice. Mix everything together until it forms a sticky, thick mixture.

Divide the mixture into 4 and form each into a burger shape. Place in the fridge for an hour to set and help secure the shape.

When ready to cook, heat the remaining oil in a griddle pan or skillet (or just use a frying pan) and place over a medium-high heat. Once hot, place the burgers in the pan and cook for 7 minutes, then flip over and cook for 5 minutes on the other side until golden brown and cooked through.

Create a burger in a bun, with fillings of your choice! **YA MON!** Enjoy.

RASTA PASTA

Here's a dish of penne pasta with a sauce made of bell peppers in Rastafarian colours, cooked down with other vegetables, herbs and spices, vegan cheese and coconut milk to make a rich, mouth-watering creamy sauce. It's **IRIE MON!** This is such a flava-filled dish that you can nyam it by itself – nothing else is needed. Super-cheap and fun to make too, it's a great way to get started in the kitchen with colourful veggies, especially for younger cooks.

SERVES 4

500g dried penne pasta

1 tbsp coconut oil

1 medium onion, diced

1 medium red onion, diced

3 spring onions, sliced

4 garlic cloves, finely chopped

1 scotch bonnet pepper, deseeded and diced

Large handful of fresh thyme sprigs

2 large tomatoes, diced

1 red bell pepper, deseeded and sliced

1 yellow bell pepper, deseeded and sliced

1 green bell pepper, deseeded and sliced

1 x 400ml can coconut milk

250g vegan cheese, grated

1 tsp salt

1 tsp freshly ground black pepper

1 tsp ground pimento (allspice)

First bring a large saucepan of salted water to the boil. Add the pasta and cook according to the packet instructions, then drain and set aside.

While the pasta is cooking, heat the coconut oil in a large frying pan over a medium heat. Add your onions, spring onions, garlic and scotch bonnet, then cook down for 5–7 minutes until the vegetables are soft.

Add the thyme sprigs, tomatoes and bell peppers and mix all the vegetables together. Now add the coconut milk and grated cheese and mix di ting!

Season with the salt, black pepper and pimento and give di ting ah mix! Simmer for a few minutes, then fold the veggies through the drained pasta before serving.

JERK-SPICED LENTIL BOLOGNESE

We used to have spaghetti bolognese every other week when we were growing up, as our mum liked to switch it up a bit, serving mainly delicious Caribbean recipes and then a few British ones (well, Brit-Italian in this case).

Truth be told, we loved the look of meaty bolognese more than the taste. We've recently adopted a more balanced diet, using plant-based ingredients such as lentils, so we thought it would be cool to tun-up the trad spag bol with some jerk seasonings. And **WOW!** This really does taste banging! The spiciness from the jerk-spiced lentils and softness of the spaghetti really complement each other, and the depth of the seasoning means the lentils have a similar flavour and texture to the beef mince of the traditional bolognese. This is a great weekday dish that doesn't take too long to cook and makes your belly full.

SERVES 4

1 tbsp olive oil

1 onion, diced

3 spring onions, sliced

4 garlic cloves, finely chopped

1 scotch bonnet pepper, deseeded and diced

2 x 400g cans chopped tomatoes

1 tsp salt

1 tsp freshly ground black pepper

1 tsp dried thyme

1 tsp ground pimento (allspice)

1 red bell pepper, deseeded and diced

2 x 400g cans green lentils, drained and rinsed

2 tbsp jerk seasoning

30g parsley leaves, chopped

320g dried spaghetti, to serve

Fresh parsley sprigs, to serve

Heat the olive oil in a frying pan and add the onion, spring onions, garlic and scotch bonnet pepper. Cook down over a medium heat for 5–7 minutes until soft, then add the chopped tomatoes and spice it up with the salt, black pepper, thyme and pimento.

Add your diced bell pepper, lentils and jerk seasoning, mix together and simmer for 10–15 minutes.

About 10 minutes before the cooking time for the bolognese is up, cook the spaghetti in a large saucepan of boiling salted water according to the packet instructions.

Drain the spaghetti and divide between serving bowls. Ladle the bolognese on top of the spaghetti and scatter over a few parsley sprigs.

RASTA ROOTS
OF VEGAN FOOD

Rastafarian culture is about a way of life and how you conduct yourself, and this includes eating 'Ital' or natural foods – food that's stripped back and connected to the land. Rastas are against processed foods made with chemicals, even preferring the natural saltiness of coconut to salt as a seasoning. The juices and fruits of Ital food come from the tropics but they resonate with the growing interest in a plant-based, vegan diet in the UK.

Shaun had experienced the Ital way of eating when he was vegan for almost a year – he really enjoyed the taste of the food, and how it made him feel. In the past, he'd been more of a meat eater, with perhaps coleslaw or steamed cabbage on the side of his plate. This shift in Shaun's diet helped us to explore lots of Jamaican veggies and fruit and encouraged us to be creative; when you eat meat, you often pay less attention to the rest of the plate. The natural tastes of plants are so vibrant and wholesome, and they lead you to a more health-conscious and balanced diet.

One of the highlights of our journey to Jamaica was a visit to a vegan Ital café run by Rastaman Ade in Negril, a chilled beach in the remote far west. They were really cool there, greeting us respectfully, *'Everyting irie, mon!'* All around were Rastas drinking the juice from fresh coconuts and eating Ital

food in a relaxed atmosphere, with the sound of the sea beyond. The people cooking at the café were knowledgeable about food, and life in general, and the place was painted with Rastafarian philosophy and pictures.

The food took a while to arrive because everything is made from scratch. It was worth the wait: the plates were a work of art, styled to perfection, a combination of plant-based flavours – plantain, rice and peas, curry tofu, stew peas and more! All delicious, and one of the best meals we had on our trip. Our driver Nigel had never experienced vegan food before, and he loved it too. He couldn't believe how good it was, because he was so used to eating meat. The imagination and creativity of their menu has been an inspiration for us back at home.

Up on Spicy Hill, where we went to visit our dad's family, we met Uncle Barrington

and saw another aspect of Rastafari and plants. He's actually a second cousin rather than an uncle, but that's the title we give him out of respect to an elder. The locals come to him as a bush doctor, for health tips and when they feel unwell. In rural Jamaica, there may not be hospitals nearby and often people use natural remedies, as well as the comfort and care of family.

Uncle Barrington has every kind of herb – for your head, throat, skin – and he talked about the natural herbs that you can put in food or drink. He showed us great bushes of long-leaved lemongrass and picked us some. 'You dry it in the breeze', he said, and then tied a small bundle into a knot for us to put into hot water to make tea. Back here in Britain, Jamaican people drink cerasee tea, made from the leaves of the bitter melon plant, as well as lemongrass, mint and other herbal teas.

Then there's 'The Herb'. Ganja grows in the ground in Jamaica like thyme or any other herb and it's legal for Rastas to use for reasons of their faith. Uncle Barrington has his likkle corner kitchen outside, where he makes ganja cake made from grated coconut and almonds fresh from the tree, leaving it to dry in the sun then packing it into small bags. After every sentence, 'Positive vibrations! Everyting irie, mon!'

Coming back, we've continued to develop favourite Ital dishes such as our Curry Tofu, Ackee and Callaloo, and also our Plantain Chickpea Curry – we make that for a lot of events as everyone loves it. This kind of food is very popular with all ages, especially in the black community where people are becoming more health-conscious about Type 2 diabetes and eating less processed food. Plant power – it's a way forward, mon!

Growing up in a Caribbean household, everyone knows that when you go to Nanny's house, you're in for a feast. Whatever the occasion, Nanny always provides the best food and drink to yuh belly full. That's after you tidy the house, wipe the floor and take your shoes off and give her a kiss before you enter the house! We've learned to cook these comforting dishes inspired by Nan, and want to share the easy and authentic food from home that we love so much – we're sure you will too. This is the chapter for Sat'day soups and stews, the hearty dishes we make at the weekend to feed family and friends. You can make them in advance so it's all easy to serve, and includes classics such as Chicken and Pumpkin Soup, Oxtail Stew and, of course, Curry Goat.

CURRY GOAT

The G.O.A.T., aka the Greatest Of All Tastes for many Caribbean food lovers. This is one of the most iconic Caribbean dishes, right up there next to jerk chicken, with the Carnival scene raising its profile around the world. If you haven't tried Caribbean food before, curry goat has to be one of the first on the list. You won't regret it. You can use either boneless goat or on the bone – we recommend with bone, to add flavour. If you really can't find goat, you can use mutton. We've given a slight twist to the traditional recipe with the addition of coconut milk – water tends to be used in Jamaica. It lifts the flavours, along with the blend of herbs and spices that infuses the meat in this soul-satisfying dish. Some people eat curry goat with rice and peas. However, a mighty army of Caribbeans believe this dish should be eaten with white rice, and white rice only! We've seen full-on arguments about this – but don't be put off, we're just passionate about our food.

SERVES 4–6

- 1.35kg goat, cut into 3–4cm chunks
- 5 tbsp curry powder
- 1 tsp salt
- 1 tsp freshly ground black pepper
- 1 tsp ground ginger
- 1 tsp ground pimento (allspice)
- 2 tsp ground turmeric
- 4 tbsp vegetable oil
- 1 large onion, chopped
- 4 garlic cloves, finely chopped
- 1 x 400ml can coconut milk
- 500ml water
- 3 spring onions, sliced
- Large handful of fresh thyme sprigs
- 8 baby potatoes, peeled and halved
- 1 scotch bonnet pepper

Put the goat in a bowl and add 2 tbsp of the curry powder, the salt, black pepper, ginger, pimento and turmeric. Cover and marinate in the fridge for up to 8 hours to get the maximum flava. Alternatively, if you have limited time, a few hours is fine.

Heat the oil in a large pot over a medium heat and add 1 tsp of the curry powder with the onions and garlic. Cook for 2–3 minutes until dark brown. We call this burning the curry, aka BUN UP di ting! Then add a likkle of the coconut milk to create a thick and tasty paste.

Add the goat to the pot and sauté until brown all over. Add half the water and the remaining coconut milk, cover and cook over a medium heat for up to 2 hours or until tender, stirring occasionally and adding 2 tbsp more curry powder halfway through. Add the remaining curry powder, to taste, and add more water during cooking if necessary.

Add the spring onions, thyme, potatoes and scotch bonnet and cook for a further 15 minutes. Remove the scotch bonnet (or leave it in longer for a spicier taste), then cover the pot and cook for 30 minutes more until the meat is very tender; it should be falling off the bone if you have used bone-in goat.

CURRY MUTTON PIE

Bringing the flava of growing up in a Caribbean household in London, we mix together curried mutton with a creamy coconut potato topping, an idea similar to the British shepherd's pie. Mutton has a similar taste to goat, and you can use either one. Baked in the oven for a crunchy finish, this dish has some unbelievable flavours! You've got to try it.

SERVES 4-6

1.4kg boneless mutton (or goat), cut into 5cm dice

1 tbsp curry powder

1 tsp each of dried thyme, ground ginger, ground pimento (allspice), salt and freshly ground black pepper

Vegetable oil

1 medium onion, diced

4 garlic cloves, finely chopped

200ml coconut milk

125ml water

Handful of fresh thyme sprigs

1 scotch bonnet pepper

2 carrots, chopped

FOR THE POTATO TOPPING

6-8 floury potatoes, peeled and cut into even chunks

125ml coconut milk

1 tbsp butter

1 egg, beaten

1 tsp freshly ground black pepper

1 tsp dried thyme

1 tsp chilli flakes

Salt

Put the mutton into a bowl and add the curry powder, dried thyme, ginger, pimento, salt and black pepper. Mix well to coat, then cover and leave to marinate in the fridge for at least 2 hours, or overnight for maximum flava.

Add the oil to a pot on a medium heat, then add the onion and garlic. Cook for 5-7 minutes until softened.

Add the mutton and brown it off for a few minutes, making sure each side takes on some colour. Add the coconut milk, water, fresh thyme, scotch bonnet and carrots and mix together. Cook for about 1½ hours until the meat is tender and falling apart.

Preheat the oven to 160°C Fan/180°C/Gas 4.

Boil the potatoes in salted water for around 15 minutes, or until tender. Drain and mash using a fork or potato masher, then add the coconut milk, butter, egg, black pepper, dried thyme, chilli flakes and salt to taste. Mix together until smooth and creamy.

Transfer the mutton to a 23 x 15cm casserole dish or a 20cm round pie dish, then top with the creamy potato mash. Spread it out evenly, then bake in the oven for about 30 minutes until the top is golden and the filling is bubbling.

STOUT STEW BEEF

Our flavalicious variation on traditional Jamaican stew beef is to use one of Shaun's favourite drinks, Dragon stout. Our Nanny McAnuff, Dad's mum, used to make stew beef all the time when we stayed round on the weekends – she'd even make it for us midweek. Our dad liked to drink Dragon Stout with it, and still does, so we've used that instead of the more usual Guinness. For those that don't know the taste, it's similar to Guinness but a bit sweeter. The beef is stewed down perfectly with wholesome veggies to make a nutritious and hearty dish, and the stout helps to **TUN UP** the flavours and create the delicious stew gravy that is best soaked up with some fluffy white rice.

SERVES 4–6

1.35kg stewing beef, cut into 3–4cm chunks

1 tsp salt

1 tbsp freshly ground black pepper

1 tbsp ground pimento (allspice)

1 tbsp browning or dark soy sauce

2 tbsp plain flour

1 tbsp olive oil, plus a little extra

1 medium onion, diced

4 garlic cloves, finely chopped

1 x 284ml bottle Dragon stout (or Guinness)

250ml beef stock

1 scotch bonnet pepper

Large handful of fresh thyme sprigs

450g baby potatoes, scrubbed and halved

4 large carrots, thickly sliced

Place the beef in a bowl, add the salt, pepper, pimento, browning or soy sauce and the flour, and mix together. Cover and marinate in the fridge for 8 hours, or overnight is even better.

Add the olive oil to a large pot over a high heat, dash in the beef pieces and sauté until brown all over. Then remove the beef from the pot and place in a bowl.

Now you will need to add a likkle more olive oil to the pot. Add the onion and garlic and cook down for 5–7 minutes over a medium heat until soft.

Add the stout and give it a stir, nuh. Now dash the beef back into your pot and mix, then add the beef stock and mix again. Add the scotch bonnet and thyme and cook until the beef is tender, about 1–1½ hours.

Take out the scotch bonnet, because you don't want it to burst! Then add your potatoes and carrots and simmer, covered, over a medium heat for 15 minutes until the vegetables are soft.

BBQ RUM RIBS

We all know sticky BBQ ribs, but who wouldn't also want a likkle bit of rum in ah it? Don't worry, it won't leave you tipsy, struggling to navigate the last bit of juicy meat-on-the-bone towards your mouth. The rum brings the BBQ flavours to life and makes them even more flavaful.

We love to tuck into these at a BBQ, and they always go quickly. You can fling dem on a grill, or easily cook them in the oven or a pressure cooker to get the lovely fall-off-the-bone effect. No matter which way, you'll be licking your fingers and craving more.

SERVES 4

700g pork baby back or individual ribs

4 spring onions, sliced, to garnish

FOR THE BBQ MARINADE

1 tsp each salt and freshly ground black pepper

1 tsp dried thyme

1 tsp ground pimento (allspice)

1 tsp chilli flakes

200ml dark spiced rum

125ml tomato ketchup

1 tbsp browning or dark soy sauce

3 tbsp cider vinegar

1 tsp Dijon mustard

50g soft brown sugar

Thumb-sized piece of fresh ginger, chopped

4 garlic cloves, chopped

1 medium onion, chopped

½ tsp freshly grated nutmeg

3 tbsp honey

Juice of 1 lime

Put all the BBQ marinade ingredients in a blender and blend until smooth.

If using a rack of pork, cut into individual ribs. Pat the ribs dry and then fling dem in a big bowl. Add the marinade and mix well to coat, then cover with cling film and marinate in the fridge overnight, or for at least a few hours.

Preheat your oven to 160°C Fan/180°C/Gas 4.

Tip the marinated ribs into a roasting tin lined with foil and arrange them meat-side down. Cook for 1½ hours, basting regularly with the marinade, until dark brown and cooked through. Garnish with the spring onions before serving.

Eat with Rice and Peas (see page 59) or Pumpkin Rice (see page 63).

If using a BBQ grill, cook for around 1¾ hours until thoroughly cooked through, basting with the BBQ sauce every 30 minutes.

PEPPER STEAK

Juicy, tender steak pieces in a tasty sauce, this is a Caribbean spin on your traditional steak fillet, with the peppered steak pieces cut up into strips, complemented by the multicoloured sweet peppers to make a real Caribbean-coloured dish – it looks so **IRIE!**

We prefer this way of cooking steak to any other because it's a very quick meal to make, with steamed vegetables and a likkle bit of potato, yam mash or rice to soak up the thick gravy.

SERVES 4

1kg steak (flank or bavette is good)

1 tsp salt

1 tsp freshly ground black pepper

1 tsp dried thyme

1 tsp paprika

1 tsp all-purpose seasoning

2 tbsp browning or dark soy sauce, plus a little extra

1 tbsp vegetable oil

1 medium onion, sliced

4 garlic cloves, chopped

1 scotch bonnet pepper, deseeded and chopped

2 tsp crushed pimento (allspice) berries

125ml beef broth (made using 2 beef stock cubes)

¼ green bell pepper, sliced

¼ red bell pepper, sliced

¼ orange bell pepper, sliced

¼ yellow bell pepper, sliced

3 spring onions, sliced

2 medium carrots, sliced

1 tbsp cornflour

Cut the steak into strips about 1cm wide. Place in a bowl and season with the salt, black pepper, thyme, paprika, all-purpose seasoning and browning or soy sauce. Cover and marinate overnight in the fridge, or for at least 1 hour.

Place a frying pan over a medium–high heat and add the oil. Add the onion, garlic and scotch bonnet and fry for 3 minutes until soft. Spoon into a bowl and set aside.

Working in batches so you don't overcrowd the pan, dash the beef strips into the same pan and brown for around 1–2 minutes on each side.

Add the pimento, beef broth, a likkle extra browning or soy sauce and the onion mixture to the beef in the pan and cook for 5 minutes. Add the bell peppers, spring onions and carrots. Mix the cornflour with enough cold water to make a paste, then add to the pan and mix well.

Leave to simmer for 5 minutes until the meat is tender.

EAT WITH Rice and Peas (see page 59), Steamed Cabbage (see page 73), Yam Mash (see page 75), white rice, mashed potatoes.

VARIATION Instead of slicing your steak, cook it whole, pan-fried in 25g butter, basting as it cooks to your preference.

NANNY'S TROLLEY

We used to pull Nanny's trolley when she went shopping – that's one way we learned about food. She always told us it's better to cook because then you know what goes into your food, plus it's cheaper. These days, Nan is always up and down shopping, and her trolley goes everywhere with her – it's almost like her protection, as it holds her up, and sometimes she leans pon it when she's tired. Here's a likkle bit of her wisdom.

'You don't want no trolley with noisy, squeaky wheels. You don't need no brake, mon – you're the brakes!'

'Frozen fish more value for money. You have to pay double for them to clean it, so do it yourself – cut the head off and take out the little parts in the centre, then wash it and put a likkle bit of salt and pepper in it. Put it in the oven to cook instead of frying – it healthy and smell less.'

'I store mi scotch bonnets in vinegar. Dem won't spoil and their strength still there. You can pour the vinegar into other dishes and get some heat, mon.'

'Put what you don't need in the freezer – hard dough bread, rice, chicken. Freeze it, mon, because you never know when you'll need it.'

'Tek the same spoon to taste tings – tip a little of the food on your hand to taste it's alrigh' but don' put the spoon back in. Not for me. That's how people get germs. No, no, no, no, no, no, no!'

'Save your plastic bags so you don't have to keep buying them – or you won't have no money left. I use them to line my wastepaper bins, then you just tek it out to the dustbin and get another.'

'Don't laugh, Shaun and Craig! Me head no come off me body yet – I'm not going to lose a screw, I'm going back to the Saviour like as how I come here!'

OXTAIL STEW

One of our favourites, this is fall-off-the-bone tender beef in a thick stew with butter beans. If you're a fan of succulent meat, we highly recommend that you try this dish.

Caribbean cooking tends to use medium-sized pieces of oxtail, which makes them easy to eat. It does take around 3 hours of cooking to achieve the melting texture you want, but if you have a pressure cooker then it cuts the time by half. When using a standard pot, be mindful to keep topping up the boiling water as necessary, so the gravy doesn't dry out in the pot.

The stew is usually eaten with white rice, rice and peas or hard food, such as boiled dumpling with yam or breadfruit.

SERVES 6

1kg oxtail, cut into medium sections

1 tsp salt

1 tsp freshly ground black pepper

1 tbsp dried thyme

5 pimento (allspice) berries

4 garlic cloves, finely chopped

2 tbsp all-purpose seasoning

2 tbsp vegetable oil

1 onion, diced

3 spring onions, sliced

1 scotch bonnet pepper, deseeded and diced

Large handful of fresh thyme sprigs

1 beef stock cube

2 tbsp dark soy sauce, Worcestershire sauce or browning

2 carrots, sliced

2 tbsp cornflour

1 x 400g can butter beans, drained and rinsed

Place the pieces of oxtail in a bowl and season with the salt, black pepper, dried thyme, pimento, half the garlic and the all-purpose seasoning. Cover and marinate overnight in the fridge.

Pour 1 tbsp of the vegetable oil into a pot over a high heat and add the oxtail pieces. Cook, turning, until brown, around 5–10 minutes, then remove to a bowl.

Add the remaining oil to the pot, then add the onion, spring onions, scotch bonnet and the remaining garlic, and sauté until soft.

Add the oxtail pieces back to the pot with the thyme sprigs. Add enough water to cover the meat, crumble in the stock cube and add the soy, Worcestershire sauce or browning. Cover and cook over a low-medium heat for 2½ hours, stirring every 30 minutes, and adding the carrots for the last 30 minutes.

Mix the cornflour with enough water to make a paste, then add to the stew and mix well to thicken. Finally, add the butter beans and cook for a further 5 minutes.

EAT WITH Rice and Peas (see page 59), Festival (see page 134) or white rice.

BULLY BEEF

Bully beef, aka canned corned beef, is one of the ultimate nostalgic ingredients for those who grew up in Caribbean households. Back in the days when saving money was a priority, corned beef was cheap, and a lot of Caribbean families were used to rustling up basic ingredients into a good meal. In Jamaica, we also heard stories from our family and locals about how they had to eat bully beef during hurricanes when they couldn't go out to the shops.

We used to get bully beef all the time when we went round to our friends' houses, or with people from church – usually in sandwiches or with rice. We loved having this version growing up and still enjoy it on a rare occasion. Funnily enough, corned beef costs a lot more nowadays. Perhaps supermarkets caught on to a growing trend within our community!

SERVES 2

2 tbsp vegetable oil

1 medium onion, chopped

4 garlic cloves, finely chopped

1 scotch bonnet pepper, deseeded and diced

250g corned beef (canned or fresh)

Large handful of fresh thyme sprigs

1 x 400g can chopped tomatoes

1 tsp all-purpose seasoning

1 tsp freshly ground black pepper

Over a medium heat, add the vegetable oil to a frying pan and wait for it to get hot, then dash in the onion, garlic and scotch bonnet and cook down for 5–7 minutes, until soft.

Add the corned beef, then start to mash down with a fork and cook until browned. Throw in the fresh thyme, chopped tomatoes, all-purpose seasoning and black pepper. Cook down and simmer for about 5 minutes until the tomatoes have reduced by a third and have a saucy consistency.

EAT WITH Fried Dumplings (see page 40), Fried Plantain (see page 37) or fluffy white rice.

STEW CHICKEN

We call this a bootleg version of the more authentic Brown Stew Chicken (see page 195) because it's cheaper to make and can feed more people. You can use skinless chicken, cut into bite-sized pieces, for an even quicker and easier dish.

SERVES 6

1.35kg bone-in chicken thighs and legs, skin removed, cut into 5cm pieces

1 tsp salt

1 tsp freshly ground black pepper

1 tsp ground pimento (allspice)

1 tbsp all-purpose seasoning

3 tsp browning or dark soy sauce

1 medium onion, chopped

1 tsp finely chopped garlic

½ red bell pepper, deseeded and sliced

½ green or yellow bell pepper, deseeded and sliced

1 scotch bonnet pepper, deseeded and sliced

Large handful of fresh thyme sprigs

2 tbsp vegetable oil

500ml water

1 tbsp cornflour

Place the chicken in a bowl and add the salt, pepper, pimento, all-purpose seasoning, browning or soy sauce, onion, garlic, bell peppers, scotch bonnet and thyme. Cover and marinate in the fridge overnight.

Add the vegetable oil to a frying pan over a medium-high heat. Take the chicken from the bowl and add to the pan. Cook, turning, for about 5 minutes until brown on each side. Remove from the pan and set aside.

Tip off half the oil in the pan and add the marinated vegetables, then cook for 3 minutes. Mix the cornflour with enough cold water to make a paste, then stir into the pan to make a gravy.

Add the chicken back to the pan, stir well and simmer for 35–40 minutes until the meat is cooked and tender.

EAT WITH Rice and Peas (see page 59), white rice or Steamed Cabbage (see page 73).

BROWN STEW CHICKEN

A succulent chicken dinner dish, this is one of our favourites on the Caribbean menu. As in other dishes, we like to marinate the meat overnight in the sauce and spices to produce an unbelievable taste that will make you say **YA MON!**

Our Nanny McAnuff would make this when we'd visit for Saturday dinners, serving it with rice and peas. The combined richness of flavours would stay on your tastebuds for the rest of the evening. We didn't manage to grab her recipe before she passed away, but the feeling that the food gave us will last a lifetime, and we wanted to try to replicate her dish. We believe we've cracked it – but we're sure she's looking down having a chuckle because we've probably missed an ingredient or two. Love you, Nanny Mac!

SERVES 4–6

- 1.8kg bone-in chicken thighs, skin removed, cut into 5cm pieces
- 1 tsp salt
- 1 tsp freshly ground black pepper
- 1 tsp ground pimento (allspice)
- 1 tsp all-purpose seasoning
- 1 tsp browning or dark soy sauce
- 2 tbsp vegetable oil
- 4 tbsp brown sugar
- 1 medium onion, diced
- 4 garlic cloves, finely chopped
- Large handful of fresh thyme sprigs
- 1 scotch bonnet pepper
- 250ml water

Put the chicken in a bowl and season with the salt, black pepper, pimento, all-purpose seasoning and browning or soy sauce. Mix up di ting, cover and marinate overnight in the fridge.

Add the vegetable oil to a large pot over a high heat and wait for di ting to get hot, then add the sugar and cook down until it turns a deep caramel colour. Add the chicken pieces and start to brown the meat on each side, coating it in the caramel.

Add the onion, garlic, thyme and scotch bonnet with the water, then give the chicken a mix up! Cook down for 30 minutes, stirring occasionally.

Remove the scotch bonnet before serving.

Rice and Peas (see page 59), white rice or Steamed Cabbage (see page 73).

CURRY CHICKEN

There are a couple of ways to make this Caribbean-style chicken curry. You can either use boneless or bone-in chicken pieces, but growing up we were taught that the bone is where the taste comes from – **DA' FLAVA!** – so we suggest using whole legs and thighs. Our nan sometimes even sucks or chews on the bone at the end of the meal for maximum taste.

As well as the flavour from the chicken, the scotch bonnet, ginger, turmeric, allspice and thyme give this tasty curry a spicy kick, while dashing in the carrots and potatoes rounds off an overall succulent dish. Perfect for all types of dinners, we remember eating this curry with some white rice or hard food on a Saturday evening.

SERVES 4

1.35kg chicken legs and thighs

4 tbsp curry powder

2 tsp ground ginger

1 tsp ground turmeric

1 tsp garlic powder

A likkle bit of salt

1 tsp freshly ground black pepper

1 tsp paprika

2 tbsp vegetable oil

1 medium onion, chopped

4 garlic cloves, chopped

1 small scotch bonnet pepper, deseeded and chopped

200ml coconut milk

1 tsp ground pimento (allspice)

4 fresh thyme sprigs

2 medium carrots, chopped

8 baby potatoes, peeled and halved

Put the chicken in a bowl and season with 2 tbsp of the curry powder, 1 tsp of the ginger, the turmeric, garlic powder, salt, black pepper and paprika. Cover and marinate in the fridge for at least 1 hour, or overnight for maximum flavour.

Pour the oil into a pot and place over a medium heat. Once hot, fry the onion, garlic and scotch bonnet for around 5–7 minutes until soft.

Add the remaining curry powder and ginger to the pot. Stir and cook for 3 minutes; this is what we call 'burning the curry'. Add a likkle water to create a creamy paste.

Add the chicken to the pot and cook until brown. Pour in the coconut milk and stir, then add the pimento, fresh thyme, carrots and potatoes. Cover and simmer for around 20–30 minutes until the chicken is tender and the vegetables are soft.

Rice and Peas (see page 59), Roti (see page 84), hard food (see page 23), white rice or with a likkle bit of coleslaw on the side – **JEEZ!**

Swap the chicken for jackfruit.

COCONUT FRIED CHICKEN

We've put our spin on fried chicken by giving it a coconut-spiced coating to make an amazing tasty dish. It's easy to make and has **NUFF FLAVA**!

SERVES 6

900g chicken legs and thighs
1 tsp salt
1 tsp freshly ground black pepper
1 tsp ground ginger
2 tbsp all-purpose seasoning
2 tbsp curry powder
1 tsp dried thyme
1 tbsp paprika
250ml coconut milk
Vegetable oil, for deep-frying

FOR THE COATING

350g plain flour
1 tsp freshly ground black pepper
2 tbsp all-purpose seasoning
2 tbsp curry powder
1 tsp dried thyme
1 tbsp paprika
2 eggs, beaten

Put the chicken pieces in a bowl with the salt, pepper, ginger, all-purpose seasoning, curry powder, thyme and paprika. Add the coconut milk, mix together and marinate for up to 2 hours.

Put the flour in a big bowl, add the dry ingredients and then beat in the eggs to make a batter. Add the chicken to the batter and mix to coat, then set aside.

Preheat the oven to 170°C Fan/190°C/Gas 5.

Heat enough oil for deep-frying in a big, heavy pan, making sure it is not more than half full. When the oil is hot enough for a piece of bread to brown in 20 seconds, about 180°C, add the batter-coated chicken, in a few batches so you don't overcrowd the pan, and deep-fry for 15 minutes until golden brown.

Drain on kitchen paper to absorb the excess oil, then place on a wire rack over a baking tray and finish in the oven for 15–20 minutes until crispy.

If you want a lighter option, instead of frying the chicken, bake it in the oven at 170°C Fan/190°C/Gas 5 for 40 minutes.

SWEET CHILLI SALMON WITH TURMERIC RICE

Sweet chilli salmon and turmeric rice all in one pot: saves time and washing-up too! This salmon recipe is something we grew up on when we were younger - our mum would often make it and we'd always look forward to it - and we've decided to complement the sweet salmon with spicy turmeric rice. This combination will have your tastebuds running wild, mon! A simple and tasty recipe for all the family to enjoy.

SERVES 4

4 salmon fillets

4 tbsp sweet chilli sauce

Juice of 1 lime

1 tbsp vegetable oil

1 medium onion, chopped

1 medium red onion, chopped

4 garlic cloves, finely chopped

1 scotch bonnet pepper, deseeded and diced

1 red bell pepper, deseeded and diced

1 green bell pepper, deseeded and diced

100g drained canned sweetcorn

1 tbsp ground turmeric

1 tsp dried thyme

250g long-grain or basmati rice, rinsed

Handful of chopped parsley

Salt and freshly ground black pepper

Put the salmon fillets in a bowl and add the sweet chilli sauce, 1 tsp salt, some black pepper and half the lime juice. Mix together, then set aside.

Pour the oil into a large, shallow frying pan over a medium heat, then add both onions, the garlic and scotch bonnet. Cook down for 5–8 minutes until softened.

Now add the bell peppers and sweetcorn and mix together. Season with salt, add the turmeric and dried thyme, then tip in the rice. Add enough water to come just above the levelled-out rice, then mix together, cover and cook for 10 minutes over a low heat. Add the salmon to the pan, cover and cook for a further 10 minutes, before serving with the parsley sprinkled over the top.

CHICKEN FRIED RICE

Caribbean-Chinese food fusions are common within the Caribbean community, and there's a big Chinese population in Jamaica. Friday nights were Chinese takeaway night growing up - chicken or prawn fried rice was always the most popular thing to get. We've created our own easy recipe using ingredients we often use at home. Save a bit of cash and have this on takeaway night instead. It'll taste even better because you've made it yourself!

SERVES 4

4 skinless chicken breast fillets, diced

A likkle bit of salt

1 tsp freshly ground black pepper

1 tbsp Chinese five-spice

3 tbsp vegetable oil

½ medium onion, diced

2 spring onions, sliced

1 scotch bonnet pepper, deseeded and diced

1 tbsp paprika

1 tbsp dried thyme

3 garlic cloves, chopped

1 tsp freshly grated ginger

2 eggs, beaten

300g mixed frozen peas and diced carrots

1 tbsp sesame oil

500g cooked white rice (around 200g uncooked)

1 tbsp butter

1 tbsp all-purpose seasoning

2 tbsp dark soy sauce or browning

Throw the diced chicken into a bowl and season with the salt, black pepper and Chinese five-spice.

Pour 1 tbsp of the vegetable oil into a frying pan or wok over a medium heat, fling in the chicken breast and cook for around 3 minutes until browned on all sides, then remove from the pan.

Pour in the remaining 2 tbsp oil, add the onion, spring onions, scotch bonnet, paprika, thyme, garlic and ginger and cook down for 5-7 minutes. Add the beaten eggs and mix, then add the frozen peas and carrots and toss around for 3 minutes.

Add the chicken back into the pan with the sesame oil and cook down for 3 minutes.

Add the cooked rice, butter, all-purpose seasoning and soy sauce or browning to the pan and stir until all the ingredients are mixed into the rice. Cook for 5 minutes over a low heat until everything is combined and warmed through.

SAFETY NOTE For food safety, cooked rice must be stored, covered, in the fridge as soon as it has cooled, then used within 2 days. When serving, make sure it is steaming hot all the way through and do not reheat more than once.

VARIATIONS Swap the chicken for prawns, or more veggies. You can also swap the rice for the same weight of cooked quinoa.

COOK-UP MACKEREL

Mackerel is complemented in this sauté with sliced onions, carrots and scotch bonnet to make a really easy and tasty dish. In Jamaica, locals who are running on a budget like to cook this and call it ghetto steak. It's our Uncle Wollie's favourite dish: *'Ya mon, we eat with nuff tings, like hard food - boiled banana, yam, dumpling or likkle bit of white rice.'*

SERVES 2

1 tbsp vegetable oil

1 medium onion, sliced

4 garlic cloves, finely chopped

1 scotch bonnet pepper, deseeded and chopped

1 x 400g can mackerel drained

1 tsp freshly ground black pepper

1 tsp ground pimento (allspice)

2 spring onions, chopped

½ red bell pepper, deseeded and sliced

½ green bell pepper, deseeded and sliced

4 fresh thyme sprigs

1 x 400g can chopped tomatoes

Pour the vegetable oil into a frying pan or skillet over a medium heat, then wait for di ting to get hot! Now add your onion, garlic and scotch bonnet and cook down until soft, around 5-7 minutes.

Now add your mackerel, break it up with a spatula and mix around. Season with the black pepper and pimento and mix up di ting. Add the spring onions, bell peppers and thyme, then add the chopped tomatoes and give di ting another mix. Simmer for 5 minutes before serving.

EAT WITH Roasted and Fried Breadfruit (see page 206).

ROASTED AND FRIED BREADFRUIT

Breadfruit brings the authentic taste of the Caribbean to almost any meal and is eaten as a starchy side dish that's similar in texture to potatoes. Available fresh in Afro-Caribbean food markets in major cities, you can also find it in a can in some supermarkets.

Breadfruit was originally treated as a good source of high-energy, nutritious food for slaves, and was brought by the British to Jamaica from the South Pacific in the eighteenth century. On our travels, we couldn't believe the amount of breadfruit we saw hanging off the trees, just ready for us to pick off and cook. Our cousin Hope and Uncle Eric tend to roast three or four at a time on the likkle coal stove in their garden, then fry one for that day and cut up the remaining ones to fling into sealable bags to store in the fridge or freezer for later. Jamaicans love freezing tings!

Here are a couple of easy and traditional ways to roast your breadfruit. You can then eat breadfruit without frying, although we prefer it fried because of the great crunchy texture and taste.

It's important to get breadfruit that is ripe and ready to roast; slightly dark marks all over it signal that it's good to go.

Firstly, cut off the stem with a sharp knife, then flip it round to the bottom side, and cut a big X into the base. This allows it to cook inside.

There are different techniques you can use to cook breadfruit, but be careful as some of these methods entail turning it over flames, so please wear oven gloves.

OVER A GAS FLAME

Turn on your gas hob to high. Wearing oven gloves, place the breadfruit base-down on top of the flame and let it roast until it turns black, then do the same on each side; this should take around 8 minutes each side, or until the whole breadfruit is roasted crispy black – a burnt-looking colour. Don't worry, it will be cooked perfectly inside.

IN THE OVEN

Rub the breadfruit with vegetable oil and roast in the oven at 180°C Fan/160°C/Gas 3 for 1½ hours until dark and steaming from both ends.

OVER A COAL FIRE

If you're cooking one breadfruit, you'll only need about two handfuls of coal. Prepare your coal on the BBQ and set it alight. Wait until the coals turn white, then, wearing oven gloves, place the breadfruit directly on the coals. Cook on each side until the whole breadfruit is roasted crispy black – a burnt-looking colour.

For all the above techniques, you'll know the roasting process is complete when the breadfruit feels 50 per cent lighter and there's steam coming out from both ends. Once roasted, let it cool down (you can speed up the cooling process by wrapping the breadfruit in a damp cloth or newspaper).

Once cool, peel off all the skin. The easiest way to do this is from the X cut upwards. Cut the peeled breadfruit in half, then cut that half in half and remove the heart. Now slice it into thick wedges. Fry the wedges in vegetable oil until golden brown on both sides.

 Ackee and Saltfish (see page 29), callaloo, as part of a Vegan Dinner Bowl (see page 161), Escovitch Fish (see page 251).

CANNED BREADFRUIT

Drain the breadfruit from the can; it should be already cut into wedges. Fry the breadfruit wedges in vegetable oil until golden. Nice and easy, mon.

BOILED BREADFRUIT

Cut thick slices off the whole breadfruit and peel off the outer skin. Remove the middle core, then cut the slices in half. Now cut the half slices diagonally into large wedge-shaped pieces. Add the wedges to a pot of boiling water and simmer for around 30 minutes until soft. Use a fork to check that it's tender, then pull it out.

CHICKEN AND PUMPKIN SOUP

'Dis soup ah cure every col' in ah yuh boddi!' One of the most-loved soups in Jamaica, this is even more appreciated in Britain when the weather takes a turn for the worse. The juicy chicken pieces make a heart-warming soup that's believed to work as a cold remedy.

Though Caribbeans include this soup in the 'Sat'day soup' category, in Jamaica it's eaten every day. You see food traders on the street with the biggest Dutch ovens, mixing together the soup, and people drinking polystyrene cupfuls during the day, even at the peak of the heat. Either way, it's a real winter warmer and something to look forward to slurping on an ice-cold winter's day – and a summer's day too!

SERVES 4–6

450g chicken legs and thighs

300g pumpkin or butternut squash, peeled, deseeded and cut into 2.5cm cubes

1 tsp each salt and freshly ground black pepper

6 pimento (allspice) berries

1 medium onion, chopped

2 spring onions, chopped

1 tsp grated garlic

1 tsp grated fresh ginger

200g sweet potato, peeled and cut into bite-sized chunks

150g yam, peeled and chopped

1 corn on the cob, sliced into chunky sections

2 medium carrots, sliced

1 cho cho (chayote), cored and diced

1 x quantity spinners (see page 126)

1 scotch bonnet pepper

4 fresh thyme sprigs

1 x 50g packet cock soup mix

Bring 1 litre of water to the boil in a large pot.

Skin the chicken and cut the legs from the thighs, if necessary. Dash the chicken into the pot, along with the pumpkin or squash. Add the salt, black pepper and pimento and cook at a lively simmer for 20 minutes over a medium heat.

Add the onion, spring onions, garlic, ginger, sweet potato, yam, corn, carrots and cho cho. Bring back to a good simmer and cook for 15 minutes.

Add the spinner dumplings, along with the scotch bonnet and thyme, and cook for a further 15 minutes, then add your cock soup mix, stir well and simmer for 5–10 minutes. Remove the scotch bonnet before serving.

PEPPER POT SOUP

A nutritious and spicy soup, this is famous for incorporating green vegetables, including callaloo. If you live near a Caribbean community you might be able to find fresh callaloo at your local veg market, or else you get it canned at a supermarket. Otherwise, it's easily replaced with spinach or kale.

Just as with red peas soup, locals in Jamaica traditionally fling in some pig tails or chicken feet to enhance the flavour. However, this is optional and we often just put in the stewing beef – or no meat at all for a delicious vegan/Ital-friendly soup.

SERVES 4

250g stewing beef, cut into 4–5cm chunks

950ml water

4 garlic cloves, finely chopped

5 pimento (allspice) berries

1 tsp freshly ground black pepper

800g fresh callaloo or spinach, or 1 x 540g can callaloo

225g pumpkin or butternut squash, deseeded, peeled and chopped

225g yellow yam, peeled and chopped

8 okra, sliced

Large handful of fresh thyme sprigs

Bunch of spring onions, sliced

1 scotch bonnet pepper

1 x quantity spinners (see page 126)

1 x 400ml can coconut milk

Put the stewing beef and water into a big pot and add the garlic, pimento and black pepper. Cook for 1 hour at a very gentle simmer until the meat is tender.

If using fresh callaloo or spinach, add it to the pot and cook until soft. Remove the callaloo or spinach using a slotted spoon and transfer to a blender (or if using canned callaloo just tip it into the blender). Blend to a purée, then pour into the pot.

Bring to the boil, then add the pumpkin or squash, yam and okra and simmer for about 20 minutes until tender. Add the thyme, spring onions and scotch bonnet, then add your spinner dumplings and simmer for about 15 minutes until cooked. Add the coconut milk, stir well and cook for a few more minutes to warm through. Remove the scotch bonnet pepper before serving.

FISH TEA SOUP

This is absolutely nothing like the tea in Britain! It's a soup much loved by Jamaicans, with their fondness for seafood. In the Caribbean, people often have their soups while on-the-go, often on the street in a polystyrene cup – funnily enough, just like takeout tea here.

For us, this is the tea of teas! Full of exotic flavours, it uses staple Caribbean vegetables such as okra, cho cho (chayote) and pumpkin, combined with fish to make a flavalicious broth.

Old-school fish tea is made with whole fish, but we hate drinking fish tea with the bones because it soon becomes pretty tiring discarding them while drinking, so instead we've used fish fillets. Just ask your fishmonger to fillet your favourite whole fish and maybe also ask for the fish heads to make a stock (see tip below).

Like in a lot of Caribbean dishes, the fish traditionally used are often the cheaper ones, such as herring or sprats. However, you can use any type of fish – for example, mackerel, snapper or cod. Just fling it in the soup and it's sure to taste fantastic.

SERVES 6

950ml water

300g pumpkin or butternut squash, peeled, deseeded and cut into 4–5cm chunks (250g prepared weight)

1 large potato, peeled and diced

5 pimento (allspice) berries

Large handful of fresh thyme sprigs

1 tsp freshly ground black pepper

8 okra, sliced

1 cho cho (chayote), cored and sliced

2 carrots, sliced

1 medium onion, diced

3 spring onions, sliced

500g fillets of fish (any type, such as mackerel or sea bass)

1 scotch bonnet pepper

1 x 50g packet fish tea mix

Bring the water to the boil in a big pot. Add the pumpkin or squash, potato, pimento seeds, fresh thyme, black pepper, okra, cho cho, carrots, onion and spring onions and cook for 20 minutes until the vegetables are tender.

Add the fish and scotch bonnet and cook for a further 10 minutes until the fish is just cooked. (If using whole fish rather than fillets, they will need to simmer in the soup for 30 minutes.) Add the fish tea mix and simmer for 1–2 minutes. Remove the scotch bonnet before serving.

FLAVA TIP If you don't have fish tea mix, create your own stock by boiling fish heads in water for 10 minutes, then straining out the bones and head.

RED PEAS SOUP

One of the traditional Jamaican Sat'day soups and definitely up there with the most-loved, this is perfect for making you feel cosy on those cold winter evenings – it's thick, warm and full of fantastic flavas.

The main ingredient is red kidney beans (yes, we know, Jamaicans often call beans 'peas' in our dishes, such as rice and peas). Stewing beef tastes absolutely delicious as the slow cooking of soup allows it to tenderise and absorb the amazing flavours in the pot. They often use chicken feet to give body to the soup in Jamaica, but thankfully this is optional and you don't have to put them in there – unless you like nibbling on those tings! We prefer to fling in chicken wings or neck, and they also give a great flavour to the soup.

In downtown Kingston we met Chef Jr, a food seller at Coronation Market, who makes this soup every Saturday, and it is one of his most-requested dishes. He gave us some really great tips, which form the basis of the recipe below.

SERVES 6-8

2 x 400g cans kidney beans

450g chicken or turkey pieces, such as neck or wings

450g stewing beef, cut into 4-5cm chunks

3 garlic cloves, chopped

1 onion, diced

3 spring onions, sliced

1 scotch bonnet pepper

4 fresh thyme sprigs

1 tsp ground pimento (allspice)

1 x 50g packet cock soup mix

1 x 400ml can coconut milk

1 sweet potato, peeled and chopped

1 yellow yam, around 300g, peeled and chopped

1 carrot, sliced

1 tsp each salt and freshly ground black pepper

1 x quantity spinners (see page 126)

Tip the kidney beans and their brine into a big pot with 2 litres of water. Add the chicken or turkey pieces and bring to the boil. Add the beef and simmer very gently for about 1 hour until the meat is tender.

Add the remaining ingredients except the dumplings and simmer for 10–15 minutes, then add the spinners to the soup and cook for 15 minutes. Take out the scotch bonnet before serving.

VEGGIE TIP Leave out the beef and chicken to make this a vegan recipe.

MANNISH WATER

This hearty soup, usually served as a starter at big parties, is traditionally made with goat's head and feet – but thankfully you can use other goat meat instead! We have had it made the authentic way, however, and loved it with goat tripe – it's totally your preference.

Within the Caribbean community, the dish has a reputation for being an aphrodisiac, hence the name Mannish Water! Filled with traditional Caribbean root vegetables, it makes a tasty winter soup.

SERVES 6–8

1 litre water

250g bone-in goat (or mutton), chopped into 6–8cm cubes

1 tsp salt

3 spring onions, chopped

Large handful of fresh thyme sprigs

1 tsp freshly ground black pepper

5 pimento (allspice) berries

4 garlic cloves, chopped

150g yellow yam, peeled and cut into 2.5cm cubes

150g sweet potato, peeled and cut into 2.5cm cubes

150g waxy potatoes, peeled and cut into 2.5cm cubes

150g cho cho (chayote), cored and chopped (optional)

400g carrots, chopped

8 okra, sliced

1 x quantity spinners (see page 126)

1 x 20g packet mannish water or cock soup mix

1 scotch bonnet pepper

Pour the water into a large pot, then add the goat and salt. Dash in the spring onions, fresh thyme, black pepper, pimento and garlic and boil up di ting over a low–medium heat for 1½ hours until the goat is tender, adding more water if necessary to keep the meat submerged.

Now fling in your yam, sweet potato, potatoes, cho cho, carrots and okra. Add the spinner dumplings to the pot and boil everyting until the yam and potatoes are soft.

Add more water, if necessary, then add the mannish water or cock soup mix and the scotch bonnet. Simmer for about another 20 minutes until the meat is falling off the bone. Remove the scotch bonnet before serving. Mannish water done!

VEGETABLE SOUP

A nutritious vegetable soup straight from the roots of Jamaica, this uses our favourite Caribbean veggies and includes a few traditional British ones as well to make a wholesome, hearty soup.

We love the natural flavours filling this big pot ah' soup and we're always picking up the bowl and pouring it down our mouths because we want to savour every last drop! **JEEZ!** It tastes good, mon!

SERVES 6

500ml water
250g split peas
4 garlic cloves, chopped
4 spring onions, sliced
5 pimento (allspice) berries, or 1 tbsp ground
Thumb-sized piece of fresh ginger, grated
30g fresh thyme sprigs
1 tbsp freshly ground black pepper
200g pumpkin or butternut squash, peeled, deseeded and diced
200g sweet potatoes, peeled and diced
200g waxy potatoes, peeled and diced
8 okra, sliced
1 x 400ml can coconut milk
280g fresh callaloo or spinach
1 scotch bonnet pepper (optional)

Firstly you'll need to grab di Dutch pot and dash in the water, along with the split peas, then bring to the boil. Add the garlic, spring onions, pimento, ginger, thyme and black pepper. Now boil di ting for about 40 minutes until the peas are soft, stirring occasionally.

Now dash in the pumpkin or squash, sweet potatoes, potatoes and okra and cook down until the vegetables are soft, around 15–20 minutes, making sure you stir the pot occasionally.

Add the coconut milk with the callaloo or spinach and stir well. If you like spice, add a scotch bonnet pepper, but remember to take it out before serving. Give the soup one more stir, then simmer briefly until the greens are wilted.

 You can add any type of vegetable you like, such as 350g chopped broccoli. Any Ital is vital!

SWEET POTATO CASSEROLE

Creamy sweet potato mash, sprinkled with cheese and baked in the oven to create a cheesy crisp topping – **JEEZ**! This recipe is inspired by our cousin Donna from Jamaica – big up cousin D! When visiting a Caribbean household for dinner, here's a tip. Always come with either a gift or dish towards the meal, or offer to help in the kitchen. There's a saying '*You come wid yu two lang han*,' which means you just came round to be given to and not give back. So we were more than happy to cook up Sunday dinner when we stayed at Aunty Eloise's family home in Kingston for the weekend. We had some more family over, including cousin Donna, who followed the Caribbean mantra and brought her signature sweet potato casserole. It tasted incredible and she kindly gave us the recipe.

SERVES 4–6 AS A SIDE

450g sweet potatoes, peeled and cut into 2.5cm cubes

160ml whole milk

2 tbsp butter

1 tsp all-purpose seasoning

1 tsp dried thyme

1 tsp paprika

1 tsp ground pimento (allspice)

1 tsp salt

1 tsp freshly ground black pepper

150g Cheddar cheese, grated

Handful of cashew nuts, crushed (optional)

Preheat the oven to 160°C Fan/180°C/Gas 4.

Add the sweet potatoes to a large pan of salted boiling water and cook until tender, around 15–20 minutes. Drain, then return to the pot and mash with a fork.

Whisk in the milk and butter and season with the all-purpose seasoning, thyme, paprika, pimento, salt and pepper, then mix together.

Pour the mixture into an ovenproof dish and sprinkle the grated cheese on top. Add some crushed cashew nuts on top as well for that extra crunch, if you want.

Bake in the oven for 20 minutes until golden brown.

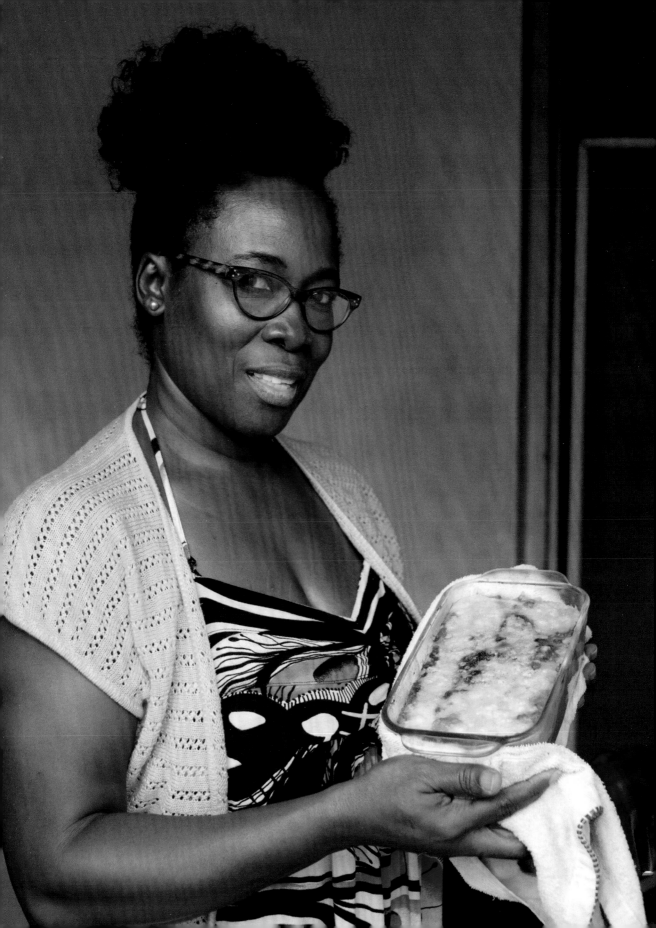

SIP
PON
IT

6

Whether the sun's shining and you're thirsty, you need to warm yourself up, or you want to celebrate and spend time with friends and family, the Caribbean has the right drink for all occasions. We love the tastes that were part of our childhood, like Carrot Juice, and other grown-up classics such as Guinness Punch. Rum will get you in the party mood, while Pineapple and Ginger Drink will help you chill out. From thirst quenchers to Carnival cocktails, get DA' FLAVA in your glass!

GUINNESS PUNCH

We love this rich, homely drink – another of Nan's specialities – not just for its taste but for the memories it brings. Nan taught us how to make it one Christmas and we've never looked back, making it for every gathering of friends or family.

In Jamaica, Guinness punch is known as a man's drink and is often sold in bars and drunk with a meal. Our granddad even used to put a raw egg in his punch!

Smooth, thick and creamy, its bitter and sweet tastes complement each other to blow your tastebuds. It's quick and easy to make – and it's pretty powerful. We remember everyone asleep on the sofa from the effects of the Guinness punch. Be easy, nuh...

SERVES 4

4 × 440ml cans Guinness

1 cup ice

1 x 400g can sweetened condensed milk or 400ml vanilla milk drink

1 tsp freshly grated nutmeg

1 tsp ground cinnamon

1 tsp vanilla extract

Blend the Guinness and ice in a blender for 2 minutes. Add the condensed milk or vanilla milk drink and stir. Add the nutmeg, cinnamon and vanilla extract, adjusting to taste. Serve in glasses topped up with more ice.

STOUT SHAKE

OMG! That's what we both said when we first sip'd pon dis drink in Jamaica. Shaun got one at the Pelican Grill in Montego Bay, and immediately said 'Bro, you gotta try it'. Craig wasn't going to turn down an alcoholic milkshake, and he loved it too. So big up the Pelican Grill! You can make the drink yourself at home with our version – it's really simple.

SERVES 2

4 scoops of vanilla ice cream

2 x 284ml bottles Guinness or Dragon Stout

Handful of crushed ice

4 tbsp chocolate syrup (optional)

Put the vanilla ice cream and Guinness or stout in a blender with the crushed ice and chocolate syrup (if using). Blend together.

RUM PUNCH: FOUR WAYS

There's nothing like a fruity rum punch at a sunny BBQ – a drink that is truly the life of the party. It's a mixture of different rums, balanced with ice-cold fruit, juiced and sliced, then dashed into a pitcher that's big enough for everyone to dive into. The third main ingredient is a strawberry-flavoured syrup that blends into the juices and gives the drink an amazing red colour. We call this drink The Silent Killer. Initially, it tastes like a harmless sweet soft drink; however, the rum is lurking in there, ready to get you later – so please drink responsibly!

This drink is such a love of ours, we've given you three other different ways to enjoy it. Give them a go, and let us know which one you prefer by tagging and messaging us on social media.

ALL SERVE 4–6

TRADITIONAL RUM PUNCH

250ml white rum

150ml dark or coconut rum

200ml strawberry-flavoured syrup (or you can use grenadine)

250ml pineapple juice

250ml orange juice

100ml fresh lime juice (from 4 limes)

Pinch of freshly grated nutmeg

Dash of Angostura bitters (optional)

Ice cubes

Slices of orange, pineapple and lime, to finish

BLUE ELECTRIC-BOLT PUNCH

200ml white rum

150ml Blue Curaçao

150ml coconut rum

600ml lemonade

150ml lime juice (from 5–6 limes)

Crushed ice

Lime wedges and a handful of blueberries, to finish

GINGER SPICE-IT-UP PUNCH

200ml white rum

200ml dark rum

600ml ginger beer or ale

1 tsp ground mixed spice

100ml lime or lemon juice, or a mixture

Crushed ice

Slices of lemon and lime, to finish

MANGO AND PASSION FRUIT TUN-UP PUNCH

250ml white rum

150ml dark rum

250ml mango juice

250ml orange juice

2 passionfruit, pulp scooped out

200ml cherry-flavoured syrup

Crushed ice

Slices of lime, mango and orange, to finish

METHOD (FOR ALL)

Pour all the punch ingredients into a large pitcher. Stir, add the crushed ice and fruit slices to finish, and sip pon it!

CARROT JUICE

Right, firstly, this is not a detox juice - far from it. It's more like a sweet and creamy milkshake. If Caribbeans did frappuccinos, this would be it. Secondly, this is Craig's favourite drink, for sure. His love for it came from spending Christmas at Nan's house, when she made it for us every year, alongside Guinness punch (which we had when we were over 18, obviously!).

As we got older, we begged Nan to show us how to make it, and this was the first recipe she ever taught us. She always used to make us do it the old-school way, grating down the carrots, then pressing and straining them to produce the juice. It's only recently that she's eased up and allowed us to use a juicer or blender, so now we have an easier and much quicker method.

This drink is definitely one to enjoy on its own - by a winter-time fire, over a game of Monopoly or dominoes - and at any time of year. The richness of the drink fills your belly, so have it by itself as a sweet treat after dinner.

SERVES 4

500g carrots, peeled and cut into chunks

1 litre water

1 x 400g can sweetened condensed milk or 400ml vanilla milk drink

1 tsp ground cinnamon

1 tsp freshly grated nutmeg

1 tsp vanilla extract

100ml white rum (optional)

1 x 284ml bottle Guinness or Dragon Stout (optional)

Handful of ice

Put the carrots in a blender or food processor. Add the water and blend until smooth.

Pour the juice into a sieve set over a jug or bowl. Squeeze and press on the carrot pulp in the sieve to get out as much juice as possible, then discard the pulp.

Stir the liquid in the jug. Add the sweetened condensed milk or vanilla milk drink, cinnamon, nutmeg, vanilla extract, white rum (if using) and Guinness or stout (if using), and stir thoroughly. Serve with ice.

VEGAN TIP For non-dairy options, use coconut milk, almond milk or soya milk in place of the condensed milk.

STRAWBERRY SKY JUICE

This traditional drink is simply a block of strawberry-flavoured ice in a bag, and is the perfect thing to have on-the-go in the baking Caribbean heat. You get people selling it on street corners in Jamaica; Craig got a craving for it in Kingston and went for it like a man finding water in a desert – so refreshing!

This really simple drink is often given to children when they're out playing, and it's popular with younger and older generations alike.

SERVES 4

1 litre water

200ml strawberry-flavoured syrup, or to taste

Pour the water and syrup into a large jug and mix. Pour individual portions into washed, clear polythene bags and place in the freezer for 24 hours.

Take out of the freezer, cut off a piece from the bottom corner of the bag, then suck pon the frozen drink.

PINEAPPLE PUNCH

Our mum tells us how Nan used to make this for her and her brothers and sisters all through their childhood, and how much she loved it. So she taught us how to make it too. The taste is similar to piña colada, but without the rum! It's a tasty mocktail for the grown-ups. But if you're bad, add some coconut rum in ah it.

SERVES 6

1.5 litres pineapple juice

1 x 400g can sweetened condensed milk

2 tbsp lime juice

1 tbsp soft brown sugar

1 tsp vanilla extract

Pinch of ground cinnamon

Pinch of freshly grated nutmeg

100ml coconut rum (optional)

Ice, to serve

Put all the ingredients except the ice into a blender and blend till smooth. Place in the fridge until ice-cold. Serve with ice.

NATURAL JAMAICAN GINGER BEER

Ginger beer was definitely one of our favourite drinks to wash down a delicious meal when we were growing up. Now we've made our own fresh version – try di ting, mon!

SERVES 2

140g fresh ginger

2 or 3 cloves

100g soft brown sugar

Juice of 1 lime

1 shot (25ml) white rum
(optional) – easy, nuh!

500ml sparkling or
spring water

TO SERVE

Handful of ice

Slices of lime

Wash and chop the ginger into small pieces (you don't have to peel it, as it will be strained out). Put it into a blender with just enough cold water to blend it to a paste. Pour into a large bowl, fling in the cloves and refrigerate overnight, or for at least 4 hours.

Tip back into the blender with the sugar, lime juice, white rum (if using), and sparkling or spring water. Blend for 3–4 minutes, then strain through a sieve. Serve with ice and lime.

Optional: to frost your glass, put some sugar on a plate, press the glass rim into the sugar and turn slightly.

DIRTY BANANA

Here's a sweet, creamy rum cocktail that you will enjoy to the max! There's nothing better than sippin' pon dis cocktail while chilling on a beach. So sit back and enjoy – it'll have you feeling irie, mon!

SERVES 2

100ml rum cream liqueur

60ml dark rum

60ml coffee liqueur

60ml milk

2 bananas, peeled

Handful of crushed ice

Put all the ingredients into a blender and blend until smooth.

PINEAPPLE AND GINGER DRINK

A refreshing sweet drink with a ginger kick, this is a traditional recipe, done the old-school Caribbean way. It's a perfect cooler on a hot day chilling in the garden, or else with your Sunday dinner, alongside some rice and peas and chicken or vegetable curry. Ya mon! Everyting nice! We've also added a quicker version if you are a bit spent for time.

SERVES 2

1 large pineapple

Thumb-sized piece of fresh ginger, chopped

1.25 litres water

Juice of 6 limes

Sugar, to taste

Honey, to taste

Ice, to serve

TRADITIONAL METHOD

Wash the pineapple well before you peel it. Cut off and reserve the pineapple skin, dice the inside (core and all) into chunks and place everything in a large bowl of water. Clean the pineapple skin and chunks thoroughly then drain, wash again, and repeat, making sure you rinse it all thoroughly.

Dash the peel and chunks into a pot, fling in the chopped ginger, add the water and boil for around 15 minutes. Let it cool for a couple of hours, then strain the liquid into a bowl.

Add the lime juice to the strained liquid, then add sugar and honey until sweetened to your taste. Strain again, stir and refrigerate until cold. Serve with ice.

QUICKER METHOD

This one is nice and easy! Prepare the pineapple as above, but discard the skin and core. Add all the ingredients to a blender and blend until as smooth as possible. Pour through a sieve into a jug and use a spatula or spoon to press down on the solids and get out as much liquid as possible. Serve with ice and sip away!

NANNY'S COLD AND FLU REMEDY

Growing up, when we had colds, Nan would be totally against giving us sachets of ginger and lemon cold remedies: she'd make her own! And it always seemed to make us feel a lot better. For the record, Nan isn't a doctor and, as far as we know, didn't ever study medicine. But we've never seen her with a cold... *Shrugs*

MAKES 1 MUGFUL

250ml water

2.5cm piece of fresh ginger, bashed

2 slices of lemon, plus the juice of ½ lemon

Honey, to taste

A likkle rum (optional)

Get a small pan, throw in the water and bring to the boil.

Add the ginger, lemon slices and lemon juice to the boiling water. Boil for 5 minutes, then strain into a mug and add enough honey to sweeten it to your taste.

Add a splash of rum if you want to... and see that cold go away!

REFRESHMENT

It's HOT in Jamaica, and all the time you need refreshment. One of the first good tings you get to chill right down is sky juice, or suck suck. It's a bit like a cross between an ice pop and a slushy. They put water and syrup into clear plastic bags and freeze them. Then you cut or bite off the end of the bag and suck it out as the ice melts in the sun and your hand. So simple!

Then there's the juice from young, green coconuts. The stall holder chops off the tip of the coconut and pushes a straw through a hole at the top. You drink it up – it's so refreshing! Once it's all finished, they crack open the coconut and you eat the inside – it's soft, like white jelly, and you scoop out the gel with a piece of the coconut shell.

We loved all the fresh, natural fruit juices in Jamaica and tried many kinds on our travels: sugar-cane juice, soursop, melon and papaya juice, and what was the ultimate Ital juice for us – pineapple, mango and melon from Rastaman Ade's café in Negril.

In our Jamaican family's homes, we witnessed how they make home-chilled drinks from scratch, such as ginger beer and pineapple ginger drink, and nothing beats drinking them with some ice in it. The ginger beer tastes nothing like the sort we get in the UK; it's more natural and you can taste the fresh root they use, whereas the canned ones popular here are fizzy. Can't lie, though – we still love the fizzy type, especially with a likkle rum!

Caribbeans love a sweet drink, such as the traditional carrot juice and Guinness

punch. Our granddad used to make Guinness punch for our mum and her siblings as children. They hated it but he'd say *'Drink it up!'* When we were growing up, Nan used to make carrot juice. So one year we decided to make it ourselves and called her up for tips – Nan makes it in a certain way and it tastes better than anyone else's. We started by grating up the carrots, but now we blend it down and then strain off the juice and that's much easier. Then we add cinnamon, vanilla extract, sweetened condensed milk, perhaps some Nrich, a vanilla milk drink. Some people add rum. The traditional way is to drink this before or after a meal, but Craig loves it any time of the day. It's usually made when you have family or friends coming round.

One drink that grows back ah yard is cocoa tea. There was lots of cocoa growing by Nanny's old house in Jamaica and our uncle showed us how they make cocoa from scratch. You grate a ball of cocoa nibs and then mix it with milk or water in a pot on the fire. It can also be sweetened with condensed milk. These balls of nibs are a big ting to bring back from Jamaica.

Another drink that grows back ah yard is sugar-cane juice. Uncle Wollie used his machete to remove the outside of the sugar cane, then cut it up into short pieces, about the length of your palm. You chew the cane, which is a bit stringy like a branch, and that's how the juice comes out. It's really refreshing, so full of natural flava that you don't need to add anything else. You find sugar cane for juice sold on street corners in Jamaica, and we can get it back home in Brixton Market too.

For another kind of refreshment, we saw nitty-gritty Kingston. Our family friend

Norris drove us to the best rum bars, called chill-out spots. They also sell beer, our favourites being Dragon Stout and Red Stripe. The Red Stripe in Jamaica tastes much crisper and refreshing – maybe it's the sun!

Before going out, the tradition is to eat some good food – hard food (see page 23) and chicken foot soup, so the rum doesn't mash you up. These bars are small street-corner places, outside, or open to the outside and perhaps by a market. The walls are painted with adverts for drinks brands such as Wray & Nephew or Appleton Rum. And the bar servers tend to be young

attractive females, so the customers, mainly men, buy more drinks, we're assuming!

The rums are either white, which are lighter in taste, or the darker aged rums. The younger people's way is to drink rum in cocktails – rum punch or rum cream cocktail, mixed with ice cream, coffee liqueur, chocolate syrup and vanilla extract. Most rum in Jamaica is over-proof – that's STRONG – the classic Wray & Nephew one is 63% ABV. Here in Britain, rum punch is the life and soul of parties we go to, everyone wants to sip pon it. There are pieces of fruit and juice in with the rum, and it's what we call The Silent Killer, because it tastes so sweet, you wouldn't think it was alcoholic – until a couple of hours later.

There are other uses for rum, too, as it's part of the life and culture of the Caribbean – you find a bottle in every Caribbean home. Mum puts it into Christmas cake, and Nan uses another kind to rub on your body and in hot drinks if you feel a cold coming on – old-school medicine! Some people even used to use it to help put the baby to sleep, back in the day.

Often as not, when you drink rum or beer in Jamaica, there's a jerk stall nearby, so you're sitting in a nice chilled spot with relaxed music. There'll be dominoes, and

alongside the music is the clacking of the pieces going down fast, with the loud 'YA MON, ME WIN!' They play the game so passionately; they're right into it, with their beers in plastic glasses perched on the corners of the table. People are just chillin', talking, laughing, playing dominoes, having banter, eating and drinking – and also drinking soup, hot soup even in the middle of the hot climate. We didn't know how they did it, but we ended up drinking it too.

You can also see how the UK urban party culture is inspired by Jamaica. But Jamaica takes it to a whole other level! We went to a party at Pier One, in Montego Bay, on a Friday night. It was ram-packed, great vibes and unison dance patterns among groups of four to six people. Once one person starts a move, you see a couple join in, and then what looks like a pre-worked dance routine. But most of the time it isn't a routine, they just flow with the vibe.

Drinks of all kinds in Jamaica are related to good times and chillin' out with friends and family, and that's the same as here in the UK. Soft or otherwise, the great thing about all Caribbean drinks is that they are really easy to make as well being tasty, and so we got plenty to sip pon and enjoy.

GET TOGETHERS

7

Growing up we learned that food was about sharing, and brought love and people together. People were hungry too, BUT it's the memories and good times made through food that are unforgettable, and those awkward family disagreements can be nudged out the way, with food as the mediator that gets us all together. Our family gatherings have certain foods that we associate with particular occasions. Sundays are about roast chicken, with our Jerk Roast Chicken giving a Caribbean lift to the traditional British lunch. Easter is for fish, and we've our favourite recipes for you to try, as well as the famous Easter Spiced Bun and Cheese that everyone loves and queues for at Caribbean bakeries. Nanny's annual birthday BBQ is a chance for a family get together and bringing out the jerk pan and the salads. Then Christmas is about eating EVERYTING! Turkey is given the jerk treatment, and with our special Honey Ham and Rum Cake, there'll be lots to enjoy throughout the holiday season. So let's get cooking and create some good times!

RED LABEL ROAST LAMB

We grew up looking forward to eating lamb on Sundays and on festive occasions, especially Easter. We hope your family and dinner guests will love this as much as ours do.

It's a juicy, roasted leg of lamb, with a spicy mint rub and a tasty gravy that includes Red Label, an aperitif much favoured in Jamaica, with flavours that blend really well with the meat and marinade. Our mum makes the most amazing roast with mint sauce, so big up Mum on this inspiration!

SERVES 8

2 tbsp olive oil

1 tsp paprika

6 pimento (allspice) berries, crushed, or 1 tsp ground

1 tsp ground cinnamon

1 tsp dried thyme

1 tbsp all-purpose seasoning

Handful of fresh mint leaves, finely chopped

Grated zest of 1 lime

1 tsp honey

A likkle salt

1 tbsp freshly ground black pepper

2kg leg of lamb

6 garlic cloves, peeled and cut into shards

3 spring onions, cut into shorter lengths

1 tbsp vegetable oil

1 large onion, chopped

A few fresh thyme sprigs

200ml Red Label wine

Put the olive oil, paprika, pimento, cinnamon, dried thyme, all-purpose seasoning, mint, lime zest, honey, salt and black pepper in a bowl and mix together.

Pierce the lamb all over using a sharp knife, then massage di seasoning mix all up in ah it. Stick the garlic shards and spring onions into the holes pierced by the knife, then wrap the lamb in foil and leave to marinate in the fridge overnight (or for at least 1 hour, if you're short on time).

Preheat the oven to 150°C Fan/170°C/Gas 3. Get a large roasting tin that will fit the lamb and place over a high heat. Pour in the vegetable oil and fling in the onion and thyme sprigs. Cook down a likkle for around 2–3 minutes, then add the Red Label wine and mix around. Unwrap the lamb and place in the tin on top of the onion. Roast in the oven for around 1½ hours or until cooked to your preference.

If you want to eat this with roasted vegetables, fling them into the roasting tin with the onion.
You can have this without the wine – just replace with beef stock and water.
Try with some Green Seasoning (see page 86).

Roasted potatoes, Yam Mash (see page 75), fluffy white rice, or Steamed Cabbage (see page 73).

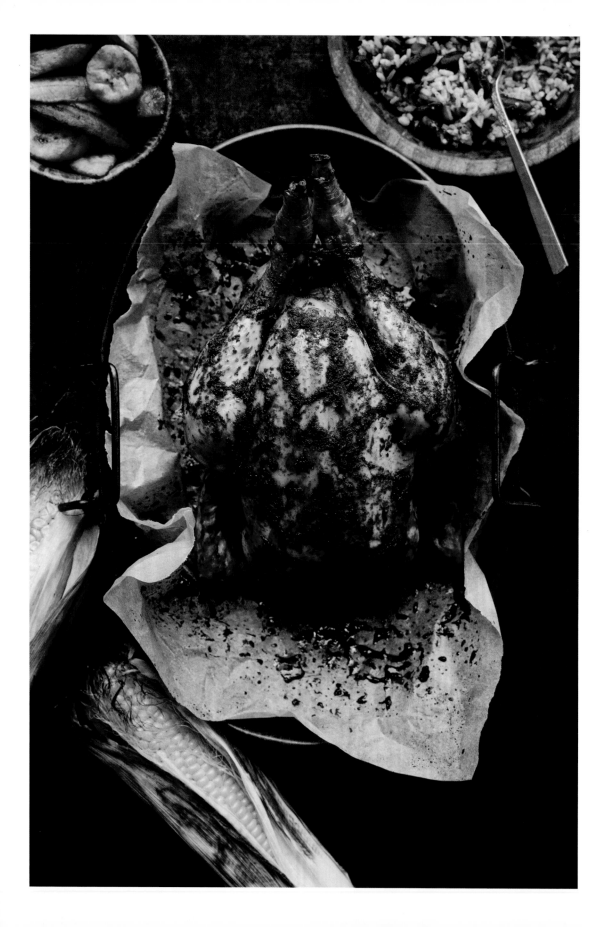

JERK-SEASONED WHOLE CHICKEN

Bring Da' Flava to your Sunday lunches with this jerk-seasoned roast chicken – and dash in some roast potatoes, rice and peas, coleslaw and mac 'n' cheese too!

Jerk is traditionally done on a jerk pan or BBQ grill. But, as you may have noticed, we don't get much BBQ weather in the UK, so we've created an oven-based recipe that you can make from the comfort of your own home. No rain inside there to interfere with your plans!

We sometimes have a whole roast chicken on Sundays and here have combined the traditional Jamaican jerk marinade with a British way of cooking. You can also use this recipe for chicken pieces – just cook them in the oven for around 50 minutes. Either way, the marinade will create a jerk-type look as the skin crisps up in the oven.

SERVES 6-8

1 chicken, about 1.75–2kg

100g butter, melted

FOR THE JERK MARINADE

1 tbsp apple cider vinegar

1 tbsp browning or dark soy sauce

1 tbsp soft brown sugar

Juice of 1 lime

1 tsp pimento (allspice) berries

1 tsp freshly ground black pepper

1 tsp ground cinnamon or freshly grated nutmeg

A few fresh thyme sprigs

2 spring onions, chopped

1 medium onion, chopped

6 garlic cloves, peeled

2 scotch bonnet peppers (tek out di seeds if you can't tek di fire)

A likkle bit of water

Start by making the jerk marinade. Put all the ingredients into a blender, and blend in short bursts until you have a thick paste.

Grab your chicken and use a sharp knife to make slashes 2cm deep over the whole thing, to ensure full flava gets into the chicken. Massage the melted butter over and inside the chicken, then pour the jerk marinade onto the meat and massage it in well. Cover and put in the fridge to marinate overnight.

When ready to cook, preheat the oven to 160°C Fan/ 180°C/Gas 4. Place the chicken in a roasting tin lined with baking parchment and cook in the oven for 1½ hours until dark brown, crispy, and cooked through – check that the juices run clear at the thickest point of a leg when pierced with a skewer or the tip of a knife. Take a look at the chicken halfway through the cooking time and if it is taking on too much colour, cover with foil.

EAT WITH Rice and Peas (see page 59) or roast potatoes.

VARIATION BBQ grill the chicken by first spatchcocking it.

FLAVA TIP For a leaner option, use chicken breast fillets.

GATHERINGS

Gatherings with family and friends bring love and so many food memories for us. During the six-week summer holidays, when Mum and Dad were working, we would stay with both our nans and spend time with our cousins, eating together and watching *Sesame Street* on the TV. We'd go shopping and watch the cooking – Granny McAnuff would put the fish on the burner to remove the scales and poke out the eyes! Nanny's Yard at Christmas was the best time – all the cousins together, eating great food around the table and playing games. This was the only time we got to use the glasses in the 'Forbidden Cabinet' (see page 55).

At Christmas time in Jamaica, families might kill a goat for the curry goat. When Craig went there before, he made friends with a goat for a week. Then one afternoon he asked, *'Where's the goat gone?'*, because it always used to make a noise outside the house. *'It's there on the table.'* They'd been given it as a gift because they had guests from London. He couldn't eat it, no way!

Another aspect of our gatherings is church. When we were growing up our local church was full of Jamaican people, even the visitors were Jamaican, so that meant the food was always good. After the service, we'd get together and have patties, chicken and rice and ginger beer. When there are functions, wedding and anniversaries, Jamaican patties ALWAYS play a part.

Cooking brings people and families together. You know what families are like – people can have their bickers – but when we gather over a meal, everyone's there, everyone's together, everything's forgotten. Food's on the table and everyone's smiling. It also gets you organised. Once you know

you've got people coming round, there's all the advance cooking and seasoning up the food so the flava gets right in overnight, and tidying up the house. Mum hoovers the place to get it tidy and clean so when people come – BOOM! They won't see Mum in the kitchen; the food's more or less done and set out already.

Christmas is now at different places but we all still get together at Nan's for her birthday BBQ every summer. She's the rock of our family and we bring out the jerk pan in her yard to celebrate. Everyone's welcome at Nanny's BBQ. This guy came to fit her new cooker once and they became close, so Nan invited him to the party. His name's Paul, and he's like family to us now. It's a very emotional time, Nanny's BBQ, because it's the only time you see all the family in one place and she is so happy. We surround the table with prayers and everyone says a speech about how precious Nanny is and how she has helped them in their lives.

In London, outside of family, the biggest gathering is the Notting Hill Carnival in

August. Carnival is typically Caribbean – people creating parties and celebrations where you get together with food and music. The anticipation builds all week. We're buying our ingredients for the rum punch, we're calling our friends, we're getting our Jamaican flags and our clothes together. We hope the sun's shining! Then we get the train and tube up and start meeting people.

With Carnival, Sunday's more for the kids as a family day and Monday's more for adults, and the whole weekend is a big vibe. The food feels like it's from the Caribbean – stalls everywhere – but varied as people come representing their different islands. The curry goat, the jerk chicken – it's AMAZING. Everyone's happy and smiling. The music, the floats, the different costumes, the feathers, the colours, the dance hall moves, hip hop, Trinidad and Tobago soca, Jamaican bashment. The islands are brought together to make Carnival music.

NANNY'S ANNUAL BBQ

HONEY-ROASTED JERK SALMON

Our spicy spin on a whole salmon is a family favourite every Christmas. It always goes quickly, so you have to be fast to get it on your plate! We don't make any regular salmon – this is our version with fragrant and delicious **FLAVA**, the marinade complementing the taste of the salmon. We love making our own jerk marinade at our family home, and neighbours knock on the door to say they can smell the spicy flavours from down the street. We use a blend of natural ingredients: onion, garlic, pimento, thyme and scotch bonnets. It's bad!

SERVES 4

1 whole salmon, about 1.5–2kg

A likkle olive oil

Handful of sliced okra

2 limes, cut into wedges

Handful of scotch bonnet peppers (optional)

4 spring onions

Handful of fresh thyme sprigs

2 garlic cloves, peeled

FOR THE MARINADE

1 tbsp apple cider vinegar

1 tbsp soft brown sugar

60ml lime juice (from 3 limes)

1 tbsp pimento (allspice) berries

1 tsp freshly ground black pepper

1 tsp ground cinnamon or freshly grated nutmeg

2 tsp fresh thyme leaves

2 tbsp chopped ginger

1 medium onion, chopped

6 garlic cloves, peeled

4 fresh thyme sprigs

2 scotch bonnet peppers, deseeded

A likkle honey

Get your fishmonger to scale and gut the salmon, or do yourself if ya bad. Use a sharp knife to score parallel lines diagonally along the fish on both sides.

Unroll a piece of foil large enough to wrap and cover the fish. Pour some olive oil on the foil, then spread out the okra, lime wedges and scotch bonnets (if using).

Put the jerk marinade ingredients into a blender and blend in short bursts until you have a thick paste.

Massage the jerk marinade into the fish, getting it right into the cuts, then place the fish on top of the vegetables in the foil. Slice the spring onions into lengths and place them inside the fish's cavity with the thyme and garlic cloves. Wrap the foil into a parcel, leaving an air space above the fish. Leave to marinate for 2 hours.

Preheat the oven to 160°C Fan/180°C/Gas 4. Place the fish parcel on a baking tray and bake for 50 minutes–1 hour until the fish is cooked through.

EAT WITH Yam Mash (see page 75) or boiled baby potatoes.

VARIATION Use salmon fillets instead of a whole salmon and pan-grill for 5–6 minutes on each side until charred and cooked to your liking.

FLAVA TIP Mix together a mango salsa to serve alongside: chopped mango, red onion, onion and avocado, with some parsley, thyme, black pepper and salt.

ESCOVITCH FISH

One of Craig's favourites, this is a beautiful, colourful dish. In Jamaica, it's traditionally made with a whole snapper but you can use other whole fish, such as red bream or rainbow fish, which is what Genna Genna, a guy we met at Hellshire Beach, Jamaica, cooked for us. Inside are many fine bones, making it all the more rewarding when you pull out a nice fleshy piece. Alternatively, use cod fillets, which are more convenient for kids and those who don't like bones.

The dish's name shows the influence of the Spanish on Jamaica, with its similarity to their dish of marinated cooked fish, escabeche. In Jamaica, you'll see people frying the fish for escovitch in a big pot, along with festival and bammy. It's quite an amazing sight, and you'll only find an experienced cook managing to do this.

SERVES 4

2 whole red snapper or any fresh fish of your choice

1 tsp salt

1 tsp freshly ground black pepper

2 tsp fish seasoning

Vegetable oil, for shallow-frying

FOR THE DRESSING

1 large onion, sliced into rings

2 medium carrots, shredded

½ medium red bell pepper, deseeded and sliced

½ medium green bell pepper, deseeded and sliced

½ medium orange bell pepper, deseeded and sliced

3 garlic cloves, chopped

1 scotch bonnet pepper, deseeded and chopped

1 tsp pimento (allspice) berries

4 fresh thyme sprigs

1 tbsp white vinegar

Ask your fishmonger to gut the fish or, if you're like our nan, do it yourself. Using a sharp knife, score parallel cuts into the fish on each side and season with the salt, pepper and fish seasoning. Season inside the fish too.

Pour enough oil for shallow-frying into a non-stick frying pan over a high heat. When hot, turn down to a medium-high heat and carefully add the fish to the oil. Cook for 10 minutes on each side until crispy and golden brown. Drain on kitchen paper to remove the excess oil.

Pour out most of the oil from the pan, then, over a medium-high heat, add the onion rings, carrots, bell peppers, garlic, scotch bonnet, pimento and thyme and cook for 3 minutes. Add the vinegar and mix together. Dash in some salt and pepper and cover the pan. Let it simmer for 5–10 minutes, or until all the vegetables are soft. Serve the fish on a plate and pour over the escovitch dressing.

Festival (see page 134), hard-dough bread or bammy.

For a lighter option, bake your fish in a 160°C Fan/180°C/Gas 4 oven for 35–40 minutes instead of frying it. Nanny does it this way, and it tastes just as good!

FRIED FISH

This is one of the go-to fish dishes at Eastertime within the Caribbean community. It's often a battle to choose between Escovitch Fish, steamed fish or this one, which is coated in a flavaful batter and deep-fried. Traditionally, it's made using pieces of red bream but you can easily use other fish, as suggested here. Jamaicans absolutely love seafood, and picking your way through bones is seen as a true art, with the enjoyment of finding the best pieces of fish. It's also known that there's more flava when the bone is in the fish. However, fillets – we like cod – are good as well, especially for those who aren't keen on bones and want to taste the amazing flavours of this dish. We love to flava up the flour too, so the outside provides a satisfying taste which complements the fish. Eaten with hard dough bread and coleslaw on the side – you can't beat it!

SERVES 4

450g cod or haddock fillets

2 tbsp each of all-purpose seasoning, fish seasoning and freshly ground black pepper

1 tbsp paprika

400g plain flour

2 eggs

125ml milk

250ml vegetable oil, for frying

FOR THE GARNISH

1 tbsp vegetable oil

1 medium onion, cut into rings

2 carrots, cut into sticks

1 each red and green bell peppers, deseeded and sliced

5 spring onions, sliced

1 scotch bonnet pepper, diced (deseeded if you like)

1 tbsp pimento (allspice) berries

½ tsp freshly ground black pepper

60ml white vinegar

Season the fillets with half of the all-purpose and fish seasonings, black pepper and paprika, then place in a shallow bowl and set aside. Add the remaining all-purpose and fish seasonings, black pepper and paprika to the flour in a bowl and mix together.

Beat the eggs in a bowl, then add the milk and whisk to combine. Pour this over the fish and let sit for 5 minutes.

Heat the oil for the garnish in a frying pan, then add the onion, carrots, bell peppers, spring onions, scotch bonnet, pimento and black pepper and mix together. Add the vinegar and simmer for 10 minutes, then set aside and keep warm.

Meanwhile, pour the oil for frying into a separate, deep frying pan over a high heat. To test when it's hot enough, slide a small piece of vegetable into the oil: if it sizzles up it's ready.

Remove the fish fillets from the milk and egg mixture and, working in batches, coat each fillet in the seasoned flour. Gently shake off the excess flour, slide the fish into the oil and fry for 5–6 minutes on each side until golden brown and crispy. Remove to a plate lined with kitchen paper to drain, and keep warm while you fry the rest. Serve with the garnish. (Illustrated over the page.)

STEAMED RED SNAPPER

One of the most satisfying dishes you'll ever have, this is a good choice for a cosy Saturday night in, as well as at the traditional Caribbean Eastertime get-together. Dis steam fish, mon! Whole snappers are steamed with some Caribbean favourite vegetables, including okra, bell peppers, potatoes and scotch bonnet. Snapper is the most popular fish to use in Jamaica, but you can use others. The fish creates a tasty broth, making this a juicy pan of flava. Traditionally, it's eaten alongside Jamaican water crackers, a piece of hard dough bread, rice, or hard food (also known as provisions).

SERVES 6

3 red snapper fish

1 tbsp all-purpose seasoning

1 tbsp fish seasoning

1 tbsp freshly ground black pepper

4–5 fresh thyme sprigs

3 spring onions

1 tbsp vegetable oil

1 red bell pepper, deseeded and sliced

1 onion, sliced into rings

3 garlic cloves, chopped

2 carrots, cut into sticks

5 medium potatoes, peeled and sliced into rounds, about 1cm thick

8 okra

1 scotch bonnet pepper, deseeded and finely chopped

2 fish tea stock cubes, dissolved in 250ml boiling water

2 large tomatoes, diced

1 tbsp butter

Ask your fishmonger to scale and gut the fish. Using a sharp knife, score 3 parallel incisions into the fish on each side.

Season with the all-purpose seasoning, fish seasoning and black pepper, massaging them over and into the fish. Place some thyme and a spring onion inside each fish and set aside.

Heat the vegetable oil in a large frying pan over a high heat. Add the bell pepper, onion, garlic, carrots, potatoes, okra and scotch bonnet, then add 60ml of the fish tea stock, the tomatoes and butter, mix and simmer for 5 minutes.

Add your fish and pour the rest of the fish tea stock on top. Cover and cook for 15 minutes over a medium heat, then serve. (Illustrated over the page.)

EAT WITH Crackers, hard-dough bread, bammy, hard food (see page 23) or white rice.

VARIATION Try any other whole fish, such as red bream, mullet or the more traditional parrot fish.

EASTER SPICE BUN

If you pass a Caribbean bakery during Eastertime, you will see a long line from inside the shop spilling onto the street – and it's usually to get this sweet bundle of joy. Similar to the British hot cross bun, this takes traditional spice-bun flavours to a whole new level. Filled with a mix of dried fruit and Guinness, alongside spices such as cinnamon and nutmeg, it has a unique taste.

The Caribbean community hold bun dear over the Easter period – though it's so good we often eat it all year round. With its sticky honey glaze, it's irresistible. Most of the time it is enjoyed with cheese as a sandwich, and our nan likes it with a cup of tea. Craig likes to toast his and then spread butter on it so it melts over the sweet, sweet, scented crispy bun. **LAWD-AH-MERCY!** It's heaven when it melts in your mouth! Whatever your preference, there's one thing that everyone agrees on: it tastes flavalicious.

SERVES 4

Vegetable oil, for greasing

300g plain flour

1 tsp each of ground cinnamon, ground mixed spice and freshly grated nutmeg

Likkle bit of salt

1 tbsp baking powder

50g butter

1 x 284ml bottle of Guinness or Dragon Stout

100ml Red Label wine or sweet sherry

150g dark soft brown sugar

1 tsp vanilla extract

1 medium egg, beaten

100g glacé cherries

130g dried mixed fruit (raisins, mixed peel, currants, etc.)

1 tbsp guava or strawberry jam

½ tbsp browning or dark soy sauce

1–2 tbsp clear honey, melted

Lightly grease a 450g/1lb loaf tin and line with baking parchment. Preheat the oven to 140°C Fan/160°C/ Gas 3.

In a bowl, combine the flour, cinnamon, mixed spice, nutmeg, salt and baking powder and set aside.

Melt the butter in a pan over a high heat, then add the stout, wine or sherry, sugar and vanilla extract. Keep stirring until it's all dissolved, then turn off the heat and leave to cool down. Once cool, add the beaten egg and stir.

Fold the flour mixture into the wet ingredients until combined, then fold in the glacé cherries and dried mixed fruit. Add the jam and browning or soy sauce, then mix together until it's a thick, sloppy consistency.

Tip the mixture into the prepared tin and bake on the middle shelf of the oven for 1 hour until a toothpick or skewer inserted into the middle comes out dry. Remove and let it cool in the tin for 1 hour, before glazing with the melted honey. **JEEZ!** Bun done!

CHRISTMAS TURKEY

Christmas time means family time – and in our family that means time to eat. We always have jerk turkey on the table around Christmas because it has so much flava. And when we describe the array of spices, herbs and scotch bonnet peppers, it leaves our friends drooling and wanting to spend Christmas with us!

SERVES 6-8

1 turkey, 4.5–5kg, with neck and giblets

Olive oil

1 x quantity Christmas Spiced Stuffing (see page 262), to serve

Vegetables of your choice, to serve

Orange slices and sage sprigs (optional), to serve

FOR THE GRAVY

750ml turkey or chicken stock

5–6 peppercorns

4–5 fresh thyme sprigs

1 bay leaf

½ orange, sliced

1 onion, peeled and quartered

2 tbsp cornflour

2 tbsp honey, or to taste

Salt and freshly ground black pepper

For your jerk marinade, add all the ingredients to a food processor or blender and blend to a paste.

Remove and reserve the turkey neck and giblets (these will be used for the gravy) and place the turkey in a large roasting tin. Drizzle with olive oil and rub it into the turkey. Massage the jerk marinade all over the skin and around the inside cavity. Leave to marinate in the fridge for at least an hour, or ideally overnight. (Remember to bring the turkey to room temperature before roasting.)

To make the gravy, put the turkey giblets and neck into a saucepan and add the stock, peppercorns, thyme, bay leaf, orange slices and onion. Bring up to the boil, then reduce the heat to a simmer. Skim off any scum that has risen to the top and simmer for 1 hour, then strain through a fine sieve. Tip the strained gravy back into the saucepan and bring back up to a gentle simmer. Mix the cornflour with enough cold water to make a paste and whisk this paste into the simmering gravy. Boil for 3–5 minutes, whisking constantly to make sure there are no lumps. Add honey, salt and pepper to taste, then leave to cool, reheating it to serve with the turkey.

When ready to roast your turkey, preheat the oven to 160°C Fan/180°C/Gas 4.

FOR THE JERK MARINADE

1 tbsp all-purpose seasoning

1 tbsp jerk seasoning

4 spring onions, chopped

Handful of fresh thyme sprigs, chopped

6 garlic cloves, chopped

5 pimento (allspice) berries

2 scotch bonnet peppers (keep the seeds in for extra spice)

1 tsp freshly grated nutmeg

1 tsp ground cinnamon

1 tbsp paprika

1 tbsp chilli powder

1 tsp sea salt

1 tsp freshly ground black pepper

1 tbsp browning or dark soy sauce

1 medium onion, chopped

1 tbsp butter, softened

A drizzle of olive oil

1 tbsp honey

Juice of ½ orange

Juice of 1 lime

Roast the turkey for 3½–4 hours. It is done when the thickest part of the leg reaches an internal temperature of between 65°C and 70°C on a meat thermometer, or when the juices from the same part run clear when pierced with a skewer or the tip of a knife. Cover with foil and rest in a warm place for 30–45 minutes.

While the turkey is resting, make and bake the Christmas Spiced Stuffing (see page 262).

Garnish the turkey with roasted slices of orange and fried sprigs of sage, if you like. Carve the turkey, then serve it with the gravy, stuffing (see page 262) and veggies of your choice. (Illustrated on the previous page.)

CHRISTMAS SPICED STUFFING

Get in the Christmas spirit with this dish! We've added a flava spin on your regular stuffing. Caution: **NUFF FLAVA**. You and your family will love it, just like we do.

SERVES 6–8

1 tbsp olive oil

20g fresh sage leaves, finely chopped

1 medium onion, diced

5 spring onions, finely chopped

6 garlic cloves, finely chopped

½ scotch bonnet pepper, deseeded and sliced (optional)

1 tsp all-purpose seasoning

2 tsp paprika

1 tsp freshly grated nutmeg

1 tsp ground cinnamon

500g pork mince

100g breadcrumbs

50g chestnuts, finely chopped

100g dried apricots, finely chopped

100g dried mango, chopped

100g fresh cranberries

1 tsp freshly ground black pepper

1 tsp salt

2 shots of white or dark rum (optional)

Pour the olive oil into a large frying pan over a medium heat. Add the sage, onion, spring onions, garlic, scotch bonnet (if using), all-purpose seasoning, paprika, nutmeg and cinnamon. Stir to mix, cook for 5 minutes and set aside.

Put the pork mince into a bowl with the breadcrumbs, chestnuts, dried apricots, dried mango, cranberries, black pepper, salt and rum (if using).

Add the sage and onion mixture to the pork mince and mix it all together until thoroughly combined. Spread out the stuffing mixture evenly in a 20cm square baking tin. Set aside in the fridge until ready to cook.

If serving the stuffing with turkey, cook the stuffing while the turkey is resting. Bake at 160°C Fan/180°C/Gas 4 for 30–40 minutes. (Illustrated on page 259.)

CHRISTMAS HONEY HAM

A traditional Caribbean Christmas dish, this tender, juicy glazed ham will have your guests drooling for more. We remember going to family functions and seeing the big pineapple rings with sweet cherries in the middle around the ham. We used to love the cherries and would pick them off and nyam them – good times! Our mum still makes this recipe on Christmas Day as our dad loves it, and so do many others. Please bear in mind that the heavier the ham you use, the longer you'll have to roast it in the oven. Enjoy, and Merry Christmas!

SERVES 8

1 gammon ham, about 2.7kg

250ml boiling water

15–20 cloves

8 pineapple rings (from a can)

8 glacé cherries

FOR THE GLAZE

250ml water

125ml orange or pineapple juice

1 tsp ground or freshly grated ginger

6 cloves

130g dark soft brown sugar

170g honey

340g guava or strawberry jam

1 tsp freshly grated nutmeg

1 tsp ground cinnamon

1 tsp all-purpose seasoning

Preheat the oven to 160°C Fan/180°C/Gas 4. Wrap the ham in foil and place in a roasting tin with a rack, with the wrapped ham sitting on the rack. Add the boiling water to the tin (this adds moisture to the ham) and bake in the oven for 2 hours.

Meanwhile, to make the glaze, pour the water into a pan over a high heat, then add the orange or pineapple juice, ginger, cloves, sugar, honey and jam. Bring to the boil, then add the remaining ingredients. Simmer for 30 minutes until reduced to a glaze the consistency of runny honey, checking occasionally to make sure it isn't reducing too fast or too much.

Take the ham out of the oven, remove the foil and then take off the skin, leaving a little bit of fat remaining on the ham. Using a knife, score parallel diagonal lines into the fat, then across to make a diamond pattern. Stud the top with the cloves.

Pour the glaze over the ham and return to the oven for 30–45 minutes until golden brown, garnishing it with the pineapple and cherries 10 minutes before the end of the cooking time. (Illustrated on page 258.)

 Rice and Peas (see page 59), fluffy white rice and gravy.

SORREL DRINK

We normally have this traditional refreshing drink during the Christmas season. It's infused with dried hibiscus petals (known as sorrel in Jamaica), ginger and other spices, with sugar to sweeten. You can also add a likkle rum, if you like. The drink is sold ready-made, but the homemade process provides the authentic, full taste. People like to make a number of bottles to give to friends and family over Christmas.

SERVES 6–8

400g dried sorrel (hibiscus flowers)

2.5 litres water

75g freshly grated ginger

5 pimento (allspice) berries

4 cloves

1 tsp ground cinnamon

Pared zest (in strips) of 1 orange

400g caster sugar

1 tsp lime juice

A likkle bit of white rum (to your preference)

Wash the sorrel and place in a large pot. Pour over the water and add the ginger, pimento, cloves and cinnamon. Bring to the boil, stirring well.

Turn off the heat after 5 minutes and then leave it to rest. Once it's cool, add the orange zest strips and place in the fridge overnight.

The next day, strain it into a bowl. You'll need to squeeze and press the sorrel remains in the sieve to get the maximum amount of juice out. Add the sugar, lime juice and rum and stir until the sugar has dissolved.

Let it rest in the fridge for a few days, then serve with ice. You'll thank us when you taste it.

CHRISTMAS RUM CAKE

This rum-infused cake is ever-present in the Jamaican household during the festive season. The soaking of the dried fruit in white rum and Red Label wine is the most sacred part. The longer you soak, the richer the taste. We make two at a time, as it keeps for months. A great dessert to share with family and friends – *but do not serve to children!*

MAKES 2 CAKES

1kg mixed dried fruit (raisins, orange peel, currants, etc.)

100ml white rum, plus a 25ml shot, and extra to finish

100ml Red Label wine

500g softened butter or margarine, plus extra for greasing

400g soft dark brown sugar

10 eggs

450g plain flour

2 tsp baking powder

1 tsp ground mixed spice

1 tsp ground cinnamon

1 tsp freshly grated nutmeg

1 tsp salt

1 tsp lemon juice

1 tsp vanilla extract

60ml browning or dark soy sauce

Glacé fruit, such as cherries, to decorate (optional)

Place the mixed dried fruit in a bowl, pour over the 100ml rum and enough wine to cover the fruit, then leave to soak overnight, or for as long as possible.

When ready to bake, preheat the oven to 160°C Fan/180°C/Gas 4. Grease 2 deep, loose-bottomed 23cm cake tins with butter and line with baking parchment.

In a large bowl, beat together the butter or margarine and the sugar until you get a creamy, fluffy consistency. (Use a stand mixer for this if you have one.) Add in the eggs one at a time, beating well after each addition, to give you a fluffy mixture.

Put the flour, baking powder, mixed spice, cinnamon, nutmeg and salt into a separate bowl and mix together. Sift the dry ingredients into the butter mixture and stir it in to incorporate. Tip in half of the soaked fruit (and any soaking liquid) and mix well until smooth. Add the lemon juice, vanilla extract, the 25ml shot of white rum and the browning or soy. Mix in the remaining soaked fruit.

Tip the mixture into the prepared tins, dividing it equally; it should come halfway up the sides (to allow the cakes to rise in the oven). Shake the tins lightly to even out the mixture. Bake in the oven for 1½ hours, until a toothpick or skewer inserted into the middle comes out dry. Keep an eye on the cakes as they bake, and if they start to brown too quickly, cover loosely with foil.

Once finished, dash a likkle more rum on the cake tops and decorate with glacé fruit or Christmas ornaments.

TOP 10 THINGS FOR A CARIBBEAN CHRISTMAS

1. Don't arrive too early on Christmas Day; there will always will be a job for you to do – cleaning, sweeping, grating carrots and nutmeg – all the longest and hardest jobs.

2. Don't try to steal meat from the Dutch pot. The sound of the Dutch pot closing is the longest and loudest sound you'll ever hear. Grandma will hear it from a mile away and she won't happy!

3. Get the best seat at the dinner table, next to the best piece of meat. You are eyeing up the chicken while the long prayers are going on and all you want to do is eat.

4. Don't give Nan too much alcohol or she'll tell all your secrets from when you were younger.

5. Do NOT enter the house/front room with your shoes on. Parents always want a clean house. No shoes to be worn in the house in case they bring in dirt!

6. Bring food containers, all shapes and sizes. It's a must at Christmas when there is always left-over food. Ice-cream containers are always used for rice and left in the freezer, so be careful if you're looking for ice cream in the freezer, you'll be in for a surprise.

7. Every Christmas Grandma will buy you the same old boxers and socks. Without fail. Just smile and act happy like it's the best Christmas present ever.

8. Make sure you line your belly and eat nuff food before you start drinking alcohol.

9. After Christmas dinner you can imagine there's a load of plates to wash up. Our dad used to always end up washing up. Make sure you have to use the toilet straight after dessert time so you avoid the washing up.

10. Never turn up unannounced. Caribbean people hate that, especially if you bring unexpected guests. Your uncle's friend's friend's mum's sister, your boyfriend's friend's mum's sister. It's a very awkward moment.

SWEET
TINGS

8

When we were well behaved as children, we'd be rewarded with a delicious sweet treat. Anyone with a sweet tooth will love these recipes, whether for a snack, a dessert or with a cup of tea. We've got sweeties such as Coconut Drops, little Jamaican pastries, the ultimate Sweet Potato Pudding and a classic crumble with a twist – this one with rum. Caribbeans have the most simple yet delicious cakes and sweet bites to make you smile, with a likkle ice cream or custard on the side, and then there's our special American-Style Cheesecake to finish off your meal with a flava explosion!

BANANA BREAD

A sweet and fluffy loaf that really does wonders to your tastebuds – like a lot of Caribbean sweet treats, we tend to eat this any time of the day! We have nuff sweet tooths! Enjoy it in the morning with a cup of tea, as our nan loves to have it, or like us for dessert with a spoonful, or four, of custard.

MAKES 1 SMALL LOAF

150g butter, softened, plus extra for greasing

4 large overripe bananas

125g soft light brown sugar

2 eggs, beaten

250g plain flour

1 heaped tsp baking powder

1 tsp ground cinnamon

1 tsp freshly grated nutmeg

A likkle bit of salt

2 tsp vanilla extract

60g raisins (optional)

Preheat your oven to 130°C Fan/150°C/Gas 2. Grease a 450g/1lb loaf tin and line with baking parchment.

Peel the bananas and fling them into a bowl. Mash them down with a masher until smooth. In a separate bowl, mix together the butter and sugar until light and fluffy (this is easier to do with an electric mixer), then mix in your eggs. Fold in the flour, baking powder, cinnamon, nutmeg and salt. Then fold in the mashed bananas, vanilla extract and raisins (if using), until well combined.

Pour the mixture into the prepared tin, evenly spreading out the top. Bake for around 45 minutes to 1 hour, until a toothpick or skewer inserted in the middle comes out clean; it's then ready to nyam.

Leave to cool in the tin for 10 minutes before turning out of the tin and cutting into slices to serve.

 For the ultimate **FLAVA** use really overripe bananas, which will give the loaf it a rich banana flavour and that authentic fluffy texture inside. Using normal bananas, it will still taste great, however!

CARROT CAKE

A soft, moist and enjoyable cake, you'll love this for its taste and also its simplicity – you may well already have most of these ingredients at home. You can serve it topped with cream cheese frosting or without. One to indulge in and enjoy with friends and family.

SERVES 12–16

A likkle butter, for greasing

350g plain flour

1 tsp baking powder

1 tsp bicarbonate of soda

A likkle bit of salt

1 tsp ground cinnamon

1 tsp freshly grated nutmeg

4 medium eggs

350g soft light brown sugar

1 tbsp vanilla extract

250ml vegetable oil

400g carrots (about 8 medium), grated

250g raisins

FOR THE FROSTING

250g unsalted butter, softened

300g cream cheese

300g icing sugar

½ tsp vanilla extract

Preheat the oven to 160°C Fan/180°C/Gas 4. Grease a 34cm x 24cm baking tin and line with baking parchment.

In a bowl, combine the flour, baking powder, bicarb, salt, cinnamon and nutmeg.

In a separate large bowl, whisk together the eggs, sugar, vanilla extract and vegetable oil using a hand-held mixer, for around 5 minutes until paler in colour.

Sift the dry ingredients into the wet ingredients and fold them in. Fold through the grated carrots and raisins until combined.

Pour the mixture into the prepared baking tin; it should be about half-full so that the cake can rise without spilling over. Place in the centre of the oven and bake for 50 minutes–1 hour until the cake is golden brown, springy to the touch and a toothpick or skewer inserted into the middle comes out clean.

Remove from the oven, leave in the tin for 5 minutes, then turn the cake out onto a wire rack and leave to cool completely.

Meanwhile, make the frosting. Beat the butter in a bowl using a hand-held mixer until pale and fluffy. Add the cream cheese and beat again until fully combined. Sift in the icing sugar and beat until the frosting is light and fluffy. Add the vanilla extract and stir to mix through.

Once the cake is completely cool, spread the frosting thickly over the top of the cake using a palette knife.

RUM, MANGO AND APPLE CRUMBLE

This one always goes down a treat when we make it for family or friends. The mango and apple are caramelised down to extract the juices, then dashes of cinnamon, nutmeg and rum lift the flavours into a fantastic-tasting dessert. You've got to try it!

This is inspired by our mum's signature dish, caramelised apple crumble – which she made with apples from Nan's back garden. It tasted great, and our dad used to request it every week. Mum has now stopped making it, as these days she's a vegan, but we've taken over with our own recipe.

This has to be one of the best desserts we've ever tried – with ice cream or custard, take your pick, but it's got to be custard for Craig, and ice cream for Shaun. As you can see in the picture, Shaun won the debate. It's all good: either option is a winner in our eyes. Let us know which one you prefer by sending your pictures to our social media.

SERVES 6–8

FOR THE CRUMBLE

400g plain flour

200g chilled butter, diced

100g soft brown sugar

45g porridge oats

100g digestive biscuits, crushed

FOR THE FRUIT

100ml orange juice

100ml mango juice

100ml apple juice

1 shot (25ml) rum

1 tsp ground cinnamon

1 tsp freshly grated nutmeg

1 tsp vanilla extract

4 red dessert apples, peeled, cored and cut into wedges (about 500g prepared weight)

500g mango flesh, cut into bite-sized pieces

Preheat your oven to 180°C Fan/200°C/Gas 6.

To make the crumble, put the flour into a bowl, add the butter and rub it in with your fingertips to create a crumbly texture. Then add the sugar, oats and crushed biscuits and mix it all together well; set aside.

Pour all the fruit juices and rum into a pan and add the cinnamon, nutmeg and vanilla. Bring to the boil, then simmer over a medium heat for 5–10 minutes until reduced by a quarter and thickened slightly.

Put the apple and mango chunks into an ovenproof dish, about 20cm x 30cm, and mix together. Pour the fruit juice mixture over the fruit and stir to combine.

Carefully scatter your crumble mixture over the top of the fruit, making sure it is evenly distributed. Bake in the oven for 35–45 minutes until the crumble topping is cooked and golden brown.

Ice cream, custard, or just by itself.

SWEET!

Jamaicans have a sweet tooth. Even our baked breads are sweet – think of bun and cheese, our Easter classic – and hard dough is another sweet bread. It's partly because we like a high density of taste: sweetness intensifies everything. That's true of savoury foods too. As the saying goes, *'The nearer the bone, the sweeter the meat'*. And sweetness is not just the literal taste; it's also a feeling of good flavours.

Our love of sweetness makes sense when you see the great variety of beautiful fruit that grows in such profusion in Jamaica, as well as the sugar cane. You want it, you pick it! Come mango season, you just scoop them off the ground too; once fruit falls from the tree, you know it's perfectly ripe. The Jamaican way to eat a mango is to peel back a likkle skin bit by bit and suck out the flesh right to the stone, rather than cutting it with a knife. You get to nyam every piece of mango this way.

When we were at Uncle Wollie's house – Nanny's Yard – we ate tangerines straight off the tree, using a huge bamboo pole with a notch carved in the top so you can get a grip on the branch. You twist it to get the fruit off. It must have been 20 foot up and everyone was shouting *'G'wan, Craig! G'wan Shaun!'* We were determined to get them down, and then we caught the fruit as it fell.

Trees and plants are part of Caribbean households in Britain – our nan's front garden and porch are full of colour and greenery all year round. People who go to the Caribbean really know about the tropical produce, because there it grows just out in the yard. They can be critical of the quality of some of the fruit sold here in the UK,

when they're tiny and don't last. Sometimes you buy fruit and leave it to ripen, and then before you know it it's rotten. Nan says fruit is supposed to stay on the tree *'until they're fit'*, and that fruit is often cut too early and young to be transported and sold all over the world *'jus to mek a likkle money'*.

Back in Uncle Wollie's garden, he also cut us some sugar cane, which is like a big, thick bamboo stick. He hacked off the skin with his machete to leave the flesh. Then you cut this into small pieces – that's how it's sold in bags at juice stalls. You chew the pieces to suck the juice out, and the natural sugar gives you so much energy you're buzzing afterwards. There's also sugar-cane tea and juice – nice and refreshing.

Uncle Barrington, the Rasta bush doctor we met, picked sweetsop off the tree. It looks like a dragon with its rough, scaly skin, then you open it up and it's full of sweet, juicy flesh. Another fruit we ate for the first time was cocoa flesh. People know all about chocolate, which is made from the cocoa pods inside. But the outside of the nib has this white, fragrant pulp that tastes a bit like lychees. YA MON! Chocolate itself isn't eaten much in the Caribbean. It's the same with

coffee, which is hardly drunk in Jamaica, but Blue Mountain coffee beans are one of the most valuable exports.

When it comes to desserts, we don't tend to do chilled ones. In a largely rural country, back in the day, people didn't have electricity and fridges. Nan tells us that when she arrived in the UK in the 1950s, she found she could set jelly by leaving it on the window ledge in her first house in London because it was so chilly. Our traditional Jamaican sweet dishes are baked in the oven and tend to have similar flavours – nutmeg, cinnamon, rum, raisins, stout. Craig's favourite is Carrot Cake and Shaun's favourite is Christmas Rum Cake. You've got to try these recipes!

As youngsters, we loved our mum's signature apple crumble, so we've used it as the inspiration for our Rum, Mango and Apple Crumble. We also remember family gatherings, and serving everyone's dessert: it was either apple crumble or rum cake with ice cream or custard. These sweet foods bring back memories of comforting times with our family, eating and laughing while watching VHS videos of Oliver Samuels, the Jamaican King of Comedy. And, still to this day, sweet treats help to create a feel-good moment.

BANANA FRITTERS

Sweet-toothers, this is for you: a finger-food treat with a soft and fluffy texture. We love to snack on these banana fritters when we feel like a sweet treat, or eat them straight out of the frying pan with some ice cream melted over them for dessert. And why not try them with a nice hot cup of tea, instead of a biscuit? Mouth-watering tings!

The smashed banana fritter mix has a hint of cinnamon and nutmeg that gives it an enriching kick that will have you drooling for more. Craig in particular loves to snack on these – he can testify how addictive they are!

SERVES 4

4 overripe bananas

120g soft brown sugar

1 tsp vanilla extract

½ tsp ground cinnamon

½ tsp freshly grated nutmeg

1 tsp baking powder

½ tsp salt

250g plain flour

80ml water

Vegetable oil, for shallow-frying

Mash the bananas in a bowl, then add the sugar and mix together. Add the vanilla, cinnamon, nutmeg, baking powder and salt and mix together. Add the flour and water, then mix well until you have a thick consistency.

Pour enough vegetable oil for shallow-frying into a large frying pan over a high heat. Using a large spoon, carefully add spoonfuls of the mixture to the pan, flattening them slightly in the pan and fitting in as many as you can without overcrowding it (you will probably have to fry them in batches).

Turn the heat down to medium and fry the fritters for 3 minutes on each side until golden brown, then transfer to a plate lined with kitchen paper to drain off the excess oil.

 Ice cream, rum cream, drizzled with honey or just by themselves.

 Use ripe plantain (so ones with lots of black spots on the skin) or sweet jackfruit in place of banana.

 If you want a healthier option, use wholemeal flour and half the amount of sugar.

JAMAICAN BANANA FRITTERS ON AN AMERICAN-STYLE CHEESECAKE

WOW, this cheesecake tastes heavenly and is one of the best desserts we've ever created. We're huge fans of this dish, inspired by the traditional version from New York, which has a big Caribbean population. The filling is whipped together with cream, bananas and other sweet gems, and layered over a crunchy crust base. After baking, the cheesecake is decorated with mouth-watering banana fritters on top. Yup, we're drooling as we speak, and we bet you are too!

SERVES 8–10

120g digestive biscuits, crushed

60g butter, melted, plus extra for greasing

FOR THE FILLING

400g full-fat cream cheese

200g soft light brown sugar

200g sour cream

100g double cream

3 eggs, beaten

1 tsp vanilla extract

100g plain flour

2 tsp cornflour

3 ripe bananas

2 tsp lemon juice

FOR THE TOPPING

1 x quantity Banana Fritter mixture (see page 283)

Vegetable oil for shallow-frying

300ml double cream, whipped to soft peaks

Handful of sliced strawberries and blueberries, to decorate

Icing sugar, to dust

Preheat your oven to 160°C Fan/180°C/Gas 4. Lightly butter a 23cm springform cake tin.

Place the crushed biscuits in a bowl and stir in the melted butter. Tip the mixture into the greased tin and spread it evenly over the base, compacting it down. Bake in the oven for 10 minutes, then leave to cool.

For the filling, combine the cream cheese and sugar in a bowl. Stir in the sour cream and double cream. Whisk in the eggs, then add the vanilla, plain flour and cornflour and mix to combine. Mash the bananas in a bowl with the lemon juice, then stir into the filling mixture. Spoon the filling over the cooled base and level it out.

Increase the oven temperature to 200°C Fan/220°C/Gas 7. Bake the cheesecake for 10 minutes, then turn down the oven temperature to 120°C Fan/140°C/Gas 1 and bake for a further 45 minutes–1 hour, or until the centre has just a slight wobble. Switch off the oven and let the cheesecake cool inside for 2 hours.

For the topping, heat vegetable oil in a pan to the depth of about 5cm. Using a tablespoon, drop walnut-sizes spoonfuls of the banana fritter mixture into the hot oil and fry for 2 minutes or until golden.

Spread the whipped cream over the top of the cheesecake. Dot the banana fritters over the cream, then scatter over the berries and dust with icing sugar.

JAMAICAN TOTO (COCONUT CAKE)

Here is the Jamaican version of the hugely popular Caribbean coconut cake - lots of the islands have a similar type of cake, with slightly different names and ingredients Caribbeans tend to go for the more simple spiced cakes, rather than anything over the top. When we were out in Jamaica, this was always mentioned when we were looking for a sweet treat. A really simple recipe that the family will love.

SERVES 10-12

200g butter, softened, plus extra for greasing
300g soft light brown sugar
1 tsp vanilla extract
3 eggs
350g plain flour
3 tsp baking powder
1 tsp ground cinnamon
¼ tsp freshly grated nutmeg
1 tbsp ground mixed spice
1 tsp ground ginger
1 tsp salt
300ml skimmed milk or coconut milk
275g grated coconut
2-3 tbsp honey, to glaze

Preheat the oven to 150°C Fan/170°C/Gas 3. Grease a 20cm x 30cm baking tin and line with baking parchment.

Using a hand-held electric mixer, beat together the butter and sugar for about 2 minutes until light and fluffy. Dash in the vanilla and then add the eggs one at a time, beating together for 3-5 minutes until paler and fluffy.

Sift the flour and baking powder into a separate bowl, then add the cinnamon, nutmeg, mixed spice, ginger and salt and mix di ting all together.

Gradually fold the flour mixture into the butter mixture until combined. Add the milk and stir in 250g of the grated coconut.

Pour the mixture into the prepared tin and sprinkle over the rest of the grated coconut. Bake for 50 minutes to 1 hour, or until a toothpick or skewer inserted into the centre comes out clean.

Remove from the oven and leave to cool in the tin for 5-10 minutes, then turn out onto a wire rack to cool completely.

To glaze the cake, gently warm the honey in a pan over a very low heat for 2-3 minutes until it is runny, then pour over the top of the cake before nyammin'.

JAMAICAN FRUIT SALAD (MATRIMONY)

Jamaican fruit salad, traditionally called matrimony, uses three fruit: orange, grapefruit and star apple. Star apple isn't always easy to find in the UK, but you can use any other peeled fruit that you have to hand instead. The nutmeg or cinnamon and the sweetened condensed milk give this dessert real Jamaican **FLAVA!** For a lighter taste, use coconut milk as a substitute. And for a stronger taste, add a splash of rum!

SERVES 6-8

3 large oranges, peeled and sliced into rounds

2 grapefruit, peeled and sliced into rounds

½ pineapple, peeled, cored and sliced

1 passionfruit, halved and pulp scooped out

1 mango, peeled and sliced

50ml dark or light rum, or strawberry-flavoured syrup (optional)

200ml sweetened condensed milk or 2 scoops of vanilla ice cream

1 tsp freshly grated nutmeg or ground cinnamon

Mint leaves, to decorate

Add all the fruit to a large bowl, pour in the rum or syrup (if using), and mix all the ingredients together gently.

Add the sweetened condensed milk or vanilla ice cream, sprinkle with the nutmeg or cinnamon, cover and chill in the fridge for at least 1 hour before serving, decorated with a few mint leaves.

To serve, spoon the fruit salad into bowls and garnish with fresh mint leaves.

VEGAN TIP

Use coconut milk or dairy-free ice cream.

PLANTAIN PANCAKES

These are American-style thick pancakes flava'd up with the ever-tasty plantain. Make sure you use ripe plantain - normal yellow plantain can be used, but the riper the plantain the sweeter the pancake will be; it's also much easier to blend down. If you want your ripe plantain to lean towards overripe, put it in a moderately hot oven for 5 minutes: you'll get the juiciest, most overripe plantain and an incredible smell too. You can add any topping of your choice, but we love these topped with sticky maple syrup and fried plantain - nice and simple, yet the most pleasurable feel-good sweet treat. Others who've tried this recipe like to add tings like blueberries and whipped cream, so have fun with it and combine your own flavas!

SERVES 6

300ml whole milk
(or almond milk)

2 overripe plantain, peeled
and chopped

30g butter, melted

2 large eggs, beaten

225g plain flour

1 tbsp baking powder

A likkle bit of salt

1 tsp brown or white sugar

1 tsp vanilla extract

TO COOK AND SERVE

Vegetable oil, for shallow-frying

4 plantain, peeled and sliced

Maple syrup

Pour the milk into a blender and add the chopped plantain, melted butter, beaten eggs, flour, baking powder, salt, sugar and vanilla extract. Blend until the mixture is thick and smooth, then let it rest for 15 minutes.

Add 1 tsp oil to a non-stick frying pan and use a piece of kitchen paper to spread it around the pan. Place the pan over a medium–high heat and, once the pan is hot, spoon in some pancake batter, allowing it to spread out to a pancake. Repeat to fit as many as you can in the pan.

Cook until set on the bottom, then flip over and cook on the other side. Repeat with the remaining batter to make the other pancakes. Set aside and keep warm.

Add enough oil to the pan for shallow-frying and turn down the heat to medium. Add the plantain slices and fry for about 2–3 minutes on each side until golden brown. Serve the pancakes topped with some fried plantain slices and a drizzle of maple syrup.

 Fried plantain, fresh fruit, or any topping of your choice.

Make the batter leaving out the plantain, then add sliced banana, strawberries or chocolate chunks before cooking, or just make them plain and add a topping.

SWEET POTATO PUDDING

Sometimes known as 'hell a-top, hell a-bottom and Hallelujah in the middle', this sweet traditional dessert with a soft inside texture is normally eaten by itself, but we love it with ice cream or custard – we're real British-Caribbean boys! In Jamaica, people often have it in the mornings before they set off for work. There is a famous pudding shop in Priory, St. Ann, where a lot of locals get their pudding, owned by 'the pudding man', aka Edgar Wallace. We went there for some great pudding, and he talked to us about the amazing recipe. And here it is, just for you guys! Straight from dung' ah yard!

SERVES 8

1 tbsp melted butter, plus extra for greasing

750g sweet potatoes, peeled and chopped into chunks

300g soft dark brown sugar

250g plain flour

200g fine cornmeal

1 tsp ground mixed spice

1 tsp freshly grated nutmeg

1 tsp salt

1 tsp baking powder

1 x 400ml can coconut milk

100g raisins or mixed dried fruit

1 tsp browning or dark soy sauce

250ml water

1 tsp vanilla extract

Preheat your oven to 160°C Fan/180°C/Gas 4. Butter a deep 23cm cake tin and line the base and sides with baking parchment.

Put the sweet potato chunks in a pan of water, bring to the boil, cook until soft then drain and mash until smooth.

While the sweet potatoes are cooking, grab a large bowl and add the sugar, flour, cornmeal, mixed spice, nutmeg, salt and baking powder, then mix together. Stir in the 1 tbsp melted butter and the coconut milk, then add the raisins or mixed fruit, the browning or soy sauce, water and vanilla extract. Add the mashed sweet potato and stir well to combine.

Pour the mixture into the prepared tin, cover loosely with foil and cook for around 1½–2 hours, until a toothpick or skewer inserted into the middle comes out clean. Let it cool down for 30 minutes before serving.

 Replace 100g of the sweet potato with 100g yam, boiling it in the same way.

COCONUT DROPS

This is a traditional Jamaican sweet snack: dry, mature coconut is cut up and boiled with ginger and sugar to make a syrup, then baked to create crunchy bite-sized treats.

We used to have this all the time from our nan, or from Jamaican 'mothers' (elderly ladies) from church as a sweet treat. They used to have a bag full of them! A really simple recipe, and guaranteed to conjure up so many nostalgic memories for people who grew up in the Caribbean or in a Caribbean household.

MAKES 20–30

350g dried coconut or
  1 whole mature (brown)
  coconut

250ml water

A likkle salt

1 tsp ground cinnamon

1 tbsp freshly grated ginger

300g soft dark brown sugar

½ tsp vanilla extract

Vegetable oil, for greasing
  (or use a silicon baking mat)

If using a whole coconut, break it open with the back of a heavy knife, or throw it onto the ground outside. Once opened, scoop out the coconut flesh and chop into fine dice. If using prepared dried coconut from a packet, just cut it into fine dice.

Pour the water into a pan and add the salt and cinnamon. Bring to the boil, then add the diced coconut, ginger, sugar and vanilla extract. Boil down until the liquid reduces to a syrup, which should take about 30 minutes. Take off the heat.

Grease a baking sheet with oil, or line it with a silicon baking mat (if you want to be really traditional, line with a banana leaf). Carefully drop tablespoons of the mixture onto the prepared sheet and leave to cool. Once cool, they are good to go!

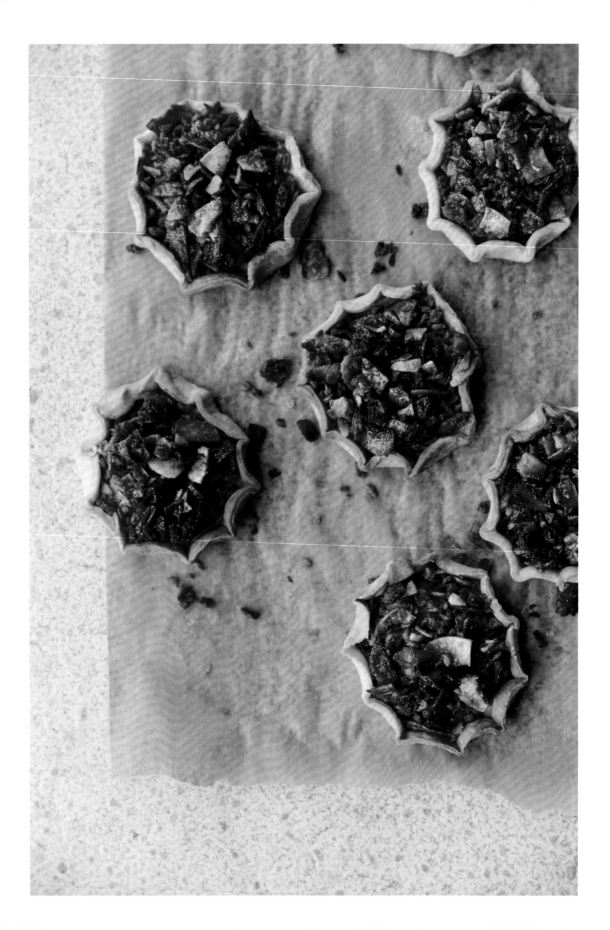

GIZZADA

Gizzada is an open tart filled with grated sweetened coconut pieces. It's fun-filled and tasty, and a favourite in Jamaica for an on-the-go sweet snack. As with a lot of Jamaican recipes, this is a recipe that came to Jamaica by the way of Portugal. Out of many, one people!

MAKES ABOUT 15

FOR THE PASTRY

500g plain flour, plus extra for dusting

100g chilled butter, diced

100g chilled shortening, diced

125ml cold water

FOR THE FILLING

300g grated coconut (from a whole coconut, see tip below, or use flakes or desiccated)

250g soft dark brown sugar

1 tsp freshly grated nutmeg or ground cinnamon

1 tbsp butter

75ml water

½ tsp salt

1 tsp vanilla extract

To make the pastry, sift the flour into a bowl and add the butter and shortening. Rub into the flour with your fingertips until the mixture is crumbly, then gradually add just enough of the water to bring the mixture into a dough. Knead briefly into a ball, wrap in cling film and rest it in the fridge for 30 minutes.

Meanwhile, for the filling, put the grated coconut, sugar, nutmeg or cinnamon, butter and water into a dry frying pan over a high heat. Mix together and simmer for 15 minutes, stirring constantly so it doesn't catch, until it has turned into a dark, sticky caramel. Stir in the salt and vanilla, remove from the heat and set aside.

Preheat your oven to 160°C Fan/180°C/Gas 4 and line a large baking tray with baking parchment.

Roll out the pastry on a lightly floured surface to about 3mm thick and use an 8–10cm plain pastry cutter to cut out circles. Use your fingers to pinch together the edges of the pastry at intervals, creating a scalloped star shape. Place on the lined baking tray and divide the filling between the tart cases, then fold the edges in a little towards the filling to create an outside ridge.

Bake for 15 minutes until the pastry is golden and cooked. Leave to cool slightly before eating warm or cold. These will keep for a few days in an airtight tin.

Use a whole mature (brown) coconut and extract the flesh the old-school way as described on page 291, then grate on a box grater – just mind your fingers!

ACKNOWLEDGEMENTS

Shaun: Firstly, I would like to thank God for making all this possible. I also have to thank our awesome nanny, for supporting us throughout this Original Flava journey from the very beginning. Thanks to our mum and dad, for letting us use their house for storage. To my fiancé, Brenda, thank you for believing in me from day one. To our brother Lewis and all my friends, thank you for your support. And not forgetting my brother Craig, my partner in crime, who has been with me on this ride, through the ups and downs, but we ride on. Love you, Bro. Thank you.

Craig: I would like to thank God, my wife Natalie for her love and support, and of course our nanny. Thanks to Mum and Dad for letting us use their house as a storage hub, and our brother Lewis. Lastly, big up to my bro Shaun – we done it, Bro! All the hard work and those long nights weren't in vain, Bruddah! Special love to our grandparents, Viola and Hugh McAnuff, who are resting in heaven.

Love to our family both in the UK and in Jamaica – thank you for making our trip around the island so enjoyable. Without all of you, this book wouldn't have been the same. Thanks to cousin Hopie, Auntie Eloise, Uncle Eric, and special thanks to cousin Laurna and Andrew for helping to organise the family links in Jamaica. Also big up to our drivers out in Jamaica, Nigel and Norris da' Bawse, who took us through every rocky hill and bush land to get us where we needed to be, along with plenty jokes and banter – you guys really made the trip unforgettable. Thanks to Moreland Primary School, for their great hospitality and allowing us to do a cooking workshop with the kids. And big up to all the street-food vendors, food shacks, veg stall owners, and people from around Jamaica for inspiring us to do this book. We're forever grateful.

We would like to give an extended thank you to the entire Bloomsbury Publishing team for all your help in taking Original Flava to di world. We're so glad to be a part of the Bloomsbury fam! Special thanks to our publisher Natalie Bellos, for believing in us and giving us the opportunity and freedom to make this dream a reality. Love ya, Nats. Thank you to Hattie Ellis for beautifully documenting our love for all things Caribbean; and to Lisa Pendreigh for working tirelessly to get the book finished. And to our publicity team, Amanda Shipp, Jen Hampson and Becky Anderson, for pushing the book to the max. To our creative dream team: Matt Russell, food and travel photographer, it was a pleasure travelling with you around Jamaica, mon. Matt, you fitted right in and now you're like family. To the lovely Polly Webb-Wilson and Hattie Arnold, thank you for your incredible dedication, for putting up with our many requests, and for your food styling skills – you both cooked like real Caribbeans in the kitchen. Big up ya'selfs! Thanks to our agent Clare Hulton. And thanks to our lil cousin Shanice for her Wonder Woman skills in making sure that our legal work is on check.

Finally, this entire dream would not have been possible without our amazing online Flava Family. You are all a big part of our journey and we would like to big up each and every one of you. You have made our dreams a reality.

BLOOMSBURY PUBLISHING

Bloomsbury Publishing Plc
50 Bedford Square, London WC1B 3DP, UK

BLOOMSBURY, BLOOMSBURY PUBLISHING
and the Diana logo are trademarks of
Bloomsbury Publishing Plc

First published in Great Britain 2019

Text © Craig and Shaun McAnuff, 2019,
written in collaboration with Hattie Ellis
Photography © Matt Russell, 2019

Craig and Shaun McAnuff and Matt Russell
have asserted their right under the
Copyright, Designs and Patents Act, 1988, to
be identified as authors and photographer
respectively of this work.

A catalogue record for this book is available
from the British Library.

ISBN: 978-1-5266-0486-6

2 4 6 8 10 9 7 5 3 1

Designer: David Eldridge
Photographer: Matt Russell
Props and Food Stylist: Polly Webb-Wilson
Assistant Food Stylist: Hattie Arnold
Project Editor: Lisa Pendreigh
Copy Editor: Sally Somers
Indexer: Vanessa Bird

Printed and bound in China by
C&C Offset Printing Co., Ltd

Bloomsbury Publishing Plc makes every
effort to ensure that the papers used in the
manufacture of our books are natural,
recyclable products made from wood grown
in well-managed forests. Our manufacturing
processes conform to the environmental
regulations of the country of origin.

To find out more about our authors and
books visit www.bloomsbury.com and
sign up for our newsletters.

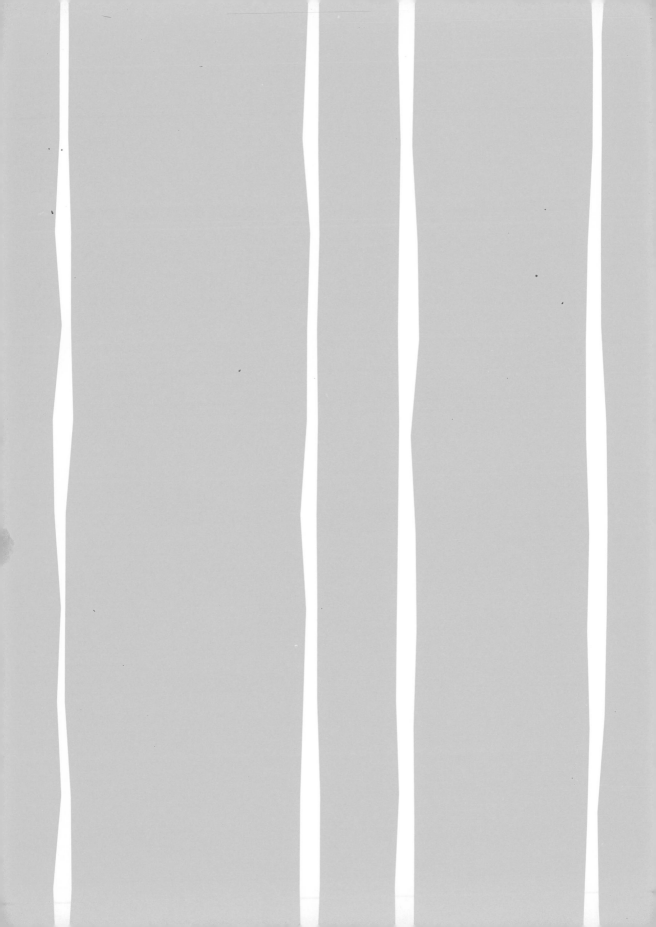